Mainstreaming and Game Journalism

Playful Thinking

Jesper Juul, Geoffrey Long, William Uricchio, and Mia Consalvo, editors

Mainstreaming and Game Journalism

David B. Nieborg and Maxwell Foxman

The MIT Press

Cambridge, Massachusetts | London, England

The MIT Press would like to thank the anonymous peer reviewers who provided comments on drafts of this book. The generous work of academic experts is essential for establishing the authority and quality of our publications. We acknowledge with gratitude the contributions of these otherwise uncredited readers.

This book was set in ITC Stone Serif Std and ITC Stone Sans Std by New Best-set Typesetters Ltd. Printed and bound in the United States of America.

Library of Congress Cataloging-in-Publication Data

Names: Nieborg, David B., author. | Foxman, Maxwell, author.
Title: Mainstreaming and game journalism / David B. Nieborg and Maxwell Foxman.
Description: Cambridge : The MIT Press, [2023] | Series: Playful thinking | Includes bibliographical references and index.
Identifiers: LCCN 2022042982 (print) | LCCN 2022042983 (ebook) | ISBN 9780262546287 (paperback) | ISBN 9780262375511 (epub) | ISBN 9780262375504 (pdf)
Subjects: LCSH: Video games—Press coverage. | Video games—Social aspects.
Classification: LCC GV1469.34.P74 N54 2023 (print) | LCC GV1469.34.P74 (ebook) | DDC 794.8—dc23/eng/20220908
LC record available at https://lccn.loc.gov/2022042982
LC ebook record available at https://lccn.loc.gov/2022042983

10 9 8 7 6 5 4 3 2 1

Contents

On Thinking Playfully

Many people (we series editors included) find video games exhilarating, but it can be just as interesting to ponder why that is so. What do video games do? What can they be used for? How do they work? How do they relate to the rest of the world? Why is play both so important and so powerful?

Playful Thinking is a series of short, readable, and argumentative books that share some playfulness and excitement with the games that they are about. Each book in the series is small enough to fit in a backpack or coat pocket, and combines depth with readability for any reader interested in playing more thoughtfully or thinking more playfully. This includes, but is by no means limited to, academics, game makers, and curious players.

So, we are casting our net wide. Each book in our series provides a blend of new insights and interesting arguments with overviews of knowledge from game studies and other areas. You will see this reflected not just in the range of titles in our series but also in the range of authors creating them. Our basic assumption is simple: video games are such a flourishing medium that any new perspective on them is likely to show us something unseen or forgotten, including those from such unconventional voices as artists, philosophers, or specialists in other industries or fields of study. These books are bridge builders, cross-pollinating both areas with new knowledge and new ways of thinking.

At its heart, this is what Playful Thinking is all about: new ways of thinking about games and new ways of using games to think about the rest of the world.

Jesper Juul
Geoffrey Long
William Uricchio
Mia Consalvo

1
Introduction: "Shall I Explain the Game?"

Whether or not you were following game-related news, early 2018 was all about *Fortnite Battle Royale*, a free-to-play shooter described as *Minecraft* (the popular open-world building game) meets *The Hunger Games* (the dystopian book and movie series). Taking inspiration from the 2017 hit game *PlayerUnknown's Battlegrounds*, developer Epic Games added the last-shooter-standing mechanic to its existing title *Fortnite*, which attracted tens of millions of players and dollars in a matter of months.[1] There is a lot to say about *Fortnite*'s instant success and how its stratospheric rise relates to the state of contemporary gaming. What interests us is the widespread coverage the game received in institutional media outlets, such as newspapers and magazines, which touched upon all the tropes typically used to discuss games and game culture. There were articles pointing towards *Fortnite*'s innovative business model and how developer Epic used "seasons" to keep players interested (and paying). Journalists pointed to not only the hundreds of thousands who watched others play on streaming platforms, the $100 million prize pool for *Fortnite*'s esports competition, and the game's cross-platform functionality, but also its ability to attract "new" groups of players, from teenagers to highly visible members of professional sports teams. A long-form article discussing many of these themes appeared in the *New Yorker*, the weekly magazine and journalistic institution (figure 1.1). In May 2018, staff writer Nick Paumgarten took an almost ethnographic approach in his attempt to make sense of how *Fortnite* "captured teens' hearts and minds."[2] His 3,680-word essay paints a comprehensive picture of both the game and contemporary game culture, attempting to contextualize *Fortnite* and make sense of its success.

What emerges from the article is an amused bewilderment matched by intense ambivalence. On the one hand, the author clearly tries to take playing *Fortnite* seriously as a meaningful cultural practice and phenomenon, given that it had already earned a spot in the pantheon of "game fads." *Fortnite*, Paumgarten observes, even offers something new: "a kind of mass social gathering, open to a much wider array of people than the games that came before." To be able to describe the game to its readers, assumed to be an audience of nonplayers, he explicitly confronts an issue that has vexed mainstream authors writing about games for decades: "Shall I explain the game? I have to, I'm afraid, even though describing video games is a little like recounting dreams." His reticence is understandable; describing

ANNALS OF GAMING MAY 21, 2018 ISSUE

HOW FORTNITE CAPTURED TEENS' HEARTS AND MINDS

The craze for the third-person shooter game has elements of Beatlemania, the opioid crisis, and eating Tide Pods.

By Nick Paumgarten
May 14, 2018

The craze has elements of Beatlemania, the opioid crisis, and eating Tide Pods.   Illustration by Ryan Johnson

Figure 1.1
Screenshot of the online version of Paumgarten's feature article on *Fortnite* for the *New Yorker*. Source: https://www.newyorker.com/magazine/2018/05/21/how-fortnite-captured-teens-hearts-and-minds.

the actual practice of playing is a thorny task. Where to begin? From what vocabulary should he draw? To grasp the game's significance, Paumgarten then engages in something akin to travel journalism, taking the reader through the rules constituting this new virtual world.

On the other hand, the author juggles the game's undeniable appeal with its inherent "wickedness." Paumgarten employs two of the oldest and most common frames used by institutional journalists covering games: characterizing play as both youthful and addictive.[3] The online version of the article's subtitle reads: "The craze for the third-person shooter game has elements of Beatlemania, the opioid crisis, and eating Tide Pods."[4] Although meant as tongue-in-cheek, it seems like the *New Yorker* editor who wrote the subtitle could not do without acknowledging the well-known "Think of the children!" rhetoric associated with game culture. It is through reputable cultural critics such as Paumgarten that those who are "not a teenager or a parent or educator of teens"—think opinion leaders, policy makers, and politicians—are introduced to a game that has "addictive power" and yet simultaneously engenders a "spirit of collaboration" and brings out "something approaching gentleness" in its players.[5]

Beyond the overnight success of another hit game, in this book we are interested in how authors—from newspaper and magazine contributors to those who see themselves as game critics and game reviewers—discuss, critique, and analyze games at a moment when they

increasingly become a *mainstream* cultural phenomenon. Paumgarten's public effort to make sense of a
supposedly novel phenomenon demonstrates the challenges of taking games seriously. How can authors speak
to a readership that skews older and upper middle class
and is unlikely to ever play anything even remotely
resembling *Fortnite*?

This effort to make sense of *Fortnite*, to explain the
game, its context of use, and its players, can be seen
as part of a broader cultural process. For us, the constant need to explain why games are worthy of attention and how they work implies that games are in a
constant state of *becoming* more mainstream. Yet, to be
very explicit about this, we do not consider games to be
mainstream at this moment in time. As such, our perspective deviates from those who are convinced that
games are already mainstream. While rarely explaining exactly what they mean by it, the journalists we
interviewed—whom we will introduce in the second
half of this book—routinely suggested that games such
as *Fortnite, Minecraft, Candy Crush Saga*, and *Roblox* have
been mainstream for a while now. After all, these titles'
successes are indicative of the massive sociocultural
and -economic pull of digital games and their ability
to be part of conversations across the pages of national
newspapers, listicles on news apps, and "longreads"
in well-respected monthly magazines. By all accounts,
most mainstream coverage acknowledges games as an
economic and, at times, creative powerhouse. But—and

this is one of the key questions we will explore—does widespread coverage equal cultural acceptance? Does a front-page feature result in a deeper understanding of why games are meaningful? Or are games increasingly visible while remaining widely vilified and misunderstood? Ask yourself: Is *Fortnite*'s coverage qualitatively like that of popular phenomena such as the FIFA World Cup, a bingeable Netflix series, or the latest Ed Sheeran single? From where we are sitting, it certainly does not feel like it.

We are deeply curious about the answer to these questions ourselves. In the first half of the book, we historicize and theorize the mainstreaming of games by accounting for the deep-rooted ambivalence that permeates game culture, player discourse, and coverage. This persistent state of uncertainty, we argue, is one of the reasons games have not been considered part of the mainstream for decades. Therefore, the source of this ambivalence warrants a survey of the game industry's and game journalism's history (chapter 2) and the evolving role of game journalists as "cultural intermediaries" or, as we call them, "passionate experts" (chapter 3). Surveying these histories sets up the book's second half, which brings us to the present. In chapter 4, we describe different kinds of game journalists and ask whether certain types allow for more meaningful game criticism. In chapter 5, we ask about the contemporary occupational and social barriers that challenge game journalists' craft. Unpacking these questions forces us to engage with the boundaries of cultural critique, journalism, and journalistic practices. This, in turn, helps us to better understand the fraught relationship between mainstreaming and game journalism. Like the opening example of *Fortnite*, in the concluding pages we argue that the challenges faced by cultural critics who want to take games seriously are manifold. Our conclusion (chapter 6) ponders potential futures: we veer between a pessimistic perspective about game journalism never reaching a more mature status and one scenario in which journalists are key contributors to the mainstreaming of games.

To work toward the second, more optimistic point, at the very end of the book we propose six rather aspirational solutions. We are under no illusion about our ability to change the current course of game coverage, whether found in mainstream outlets, among streamers, or in niche publications. Critics such as Paumgarten, who thread the needle between serious cultural critique and deep-rooted self-deprecation, are likely to remain the norm. Rather, our review of past and present modes of game reportage is meant to offer fertile ground for future conversations. For those who have made attempts to write about games in a meaningful way, or for those who might, we aim to offer insight into decades-long struggles and present preoccupations among game critics. Just as the game industry seems to lack an institutional memory, we have seen the same conversations, themes, and frustrations voiced by game journalists time and again.[6] Documenting some of these themes and tropes may help us to advance collective discussions about the mainstreaming of games vis-à-vis game journalism.

Before we revisit the past in the next chapter, however, let us spend a bit more time fleshing out the two main conceptual parts of our argument: First, the deep sense of ambivalence underlying game culture, criticism, and coverage, along with a reflection on key terms and concepts related to game journalism and its boundaries; and second—the linchpin of our argument—the notion of mainstreaming itself.

Game Culture's Constitutive Ambivalences

Game culture has always been—and remains, we believe —one of stark divisions: you are either an outspoken supporter of gaming or vehemently against it. If you are a parent, you may be constantly worried: "Should my child play so much *Fortnite*?" If you are a US politician or TV host, you may forgo sensible gun laws and instead be tempted to blame "violent games" after yet another school shooting. On the other side of the spectrum, we see self-proclaimed gamers who are sick and tired of all those who constantly express unfounded negative opinions. "They"—parents, pundits, and politicians—just do not "get it." So frustrating! Do they even play games? Probably not. The psychologists

Andrew Przybylski and Netta Weinstein found that negative opinions about games and their theoretical connection to violence are most prominent among those who have "little direct exposure to electronic gaming contexts."[7]

There are several historical, social, and cultural reasons at the heart of these baked-in tensions. One particularly persistent frame popped up in our *Fortnite* example: games are perceived as child's play. Even though many games are marketed to adults, as a cultural practice, digital play has a very hard time shaking its youthful image. The second dominant frame is that games are always meant to be "fun" or entertaining. Because they are explicitly hailed as for-profit products, makers face forceful pushback when they want to engage with meaningful themes or controversial issues. For many, it still is difficult to imagine a blockbuster game centered on immigration, the Holocaust, or cancer. As many players and game critics will be eager to tell you, a handful of games with such themes do exist, but do we consider them part of mainstream game culture?[8] Developers of such "controversial" games go out of their way to stress that they "don't necessarily see entertainment as their objective—the point is to give people something to think about, maybe even educate them."[9] Framing games as educational gives developers a bit more leeway, but only so much. Despite such efforts, digital play still "subsists in a culture that fundamentally disapproves of it."[10]

Thus, to understand contemporary game culture is to come to terms with a great many "unresolved contradictions."[11] In a series of books and articles, the sociologist Graeme Kirkpatrick analyzes these tensions, noting that game culture is marked by a series of "constitutive ambivalences." He contends that "computer games are more than just games, but they do not become art; gaming is pleasurable and harmless yet also 'addictive' and, on occasion, 'not normal,' and, finally, games are not suitable for children, yet they continue to be fundamentally childish."[12] In the United States, mainstream conversations about gaming are marked by constant concerns about addiction and play being a wasteful activity.[13] At the same time, however, there is an acute awareness of the game industry's vitality. This back-and-forth, often within the same article or even paragraph, is an ongoing discursive battle among worried parents, policy makers, players, journalists, game critics, and dedicated fans that has persisted for decades. From the 1980s onwards, magazines, newspapers, and specialist game outlets all have been foundational in the social construction of digital games and players. Therefore, we are particularly interested in both the role that game journalists play in creating and sustaining these contradictions, and in their apparent inability to move beyond them.

As with so many issues and questions we explore in the book, this deep sense of ambivalence is not unique to games. In their ethnographic account of "collective online spaces," such as Twitter, YouTube, Reddit, and 4chan, the digital culture scholars Whitney Phillips and Ryan Milner point toward these places as "simultaneously antagonistic and social, creative and disruptive, humorous and barbed."[14] Driven by the popularity principle, advertising-driven platforms such as Facebook, Twitter, and TikTok tend to favor memetic, affective content over deliberation and reflection, thereby sharpening existing divides rather than bringing (sub) cultures together.[15] The same could be said of game culture. To some this might be utterly unsurprising. There is a clear overlap between game spaces and online platforms, their inhabitants, and their practices because players use these platforms to watch, critique, and debate games. The most dedicated parts of game culture thrive in broader online communities that are clearly playful and creative while simultaneously displaying a decidedly nihilistic, sometimes outright violent streak.[16]

Collectively, the "constitutive ambivalences" highlighted by Kirkpatrick involve a wide range of actors, each with different motivations and agendas. We have been mindful of this plurality of voices when we question how game coverage interacts with the perennial clash between digital play's outspoken proponents, many of whom invest substantial time and money in their favorite pastime, and opponents who are forever fearful of addiction, aggression, displacement, and other harmful effects ascribed to excessive gameplay.

Game Journalism: Institutional Journalists, Game Reviewers, and Critics

What, then, counts as game journalism? We will use it as an umbrella term that covers all those who engage in the professional practice of writing and publishing about games. This includes not only staff writers, editors, reporters, and freelancers, but also interns and unpaid volunteers working for for-profit outlets. Together, they draw from a range of occupational labels: journalist, critic, reviewer, streamer, or blogger. Put differently, ask ten different writers how they see themselves and you will get ten different answers.[17] Ask them what their job entails, and it gets even more complicated. Ask them what they think their colleagues do—in terms of occupational best practices—and all bets are off. The deep-rooted ambiguity and uncertainty that permeates game culture has clearly rubbed off on the self-perception of those who cover it.[18]

Game journalists' inherent introspection leads to recurring conversations about who to include and exclude in the pantheon of game journalism, thereby demarcating one's territory and legitimizing one's own role. In journalism studies, this constant process of justification and reflection is known as "boundary work," or the daily "codification and legitimation" of who is "in" and who is "out" of the professional field.[19] Performing boundary work is by no means unique to those who write about games, nor is it unique to journalism, yet it helps to legitimize a reporter's "gatekeeping" function—their ability to choose the content and nature of messages disseminated to the wider public.[20] It can also work the other way around. By purposely stepping outside existing institutional and occupational boundaries, game writers can act more freely—or, in some cases, abdicate responsibility for a failure or unwillingness to uphold professional values, such as objective reporting or resisting commercial influence.

Understanding boundary work allows us to distinguish between the different groups of game writers. In this book, we identify three types (table 1)—*institutional journalists*, *game reviewers*, and *game critics*—noting that our focus in the first half of the book is on the written word rather than audio (e.g., podcasting, radio), photography, or video (e.g., vlogging, streaming, or TV) coverage. In the second half of the book, we consider emerging reporting practices, particularly video and live streaming. Throughout we remain focused on professionals, meaning that we purposely left out online critics and reviewers in their role as "private citizens–customers," whom Maarit Jaakkola calls "vernacular amateurs."[21] Our typology of writers, therefore, presents ideal types to serve our analysis; members of each group largely avoid (if not openly resist) occupational categorizations.[22] We pursued this scheme to engage with the persistent ambivalence among authors themselves about their craft. As we will explain, even though each group performs boundary work differently, there

Table 1
Types of Game Journalists

Journalist Type	Occupational Equivalents	Scholarly Classification
Institutional journalists	Beat reporters affiliated with newspapers and magazines	Journalism
Game reviewers	Travel and fashion journalists, food critics, and other forms of service journalism	Lifestyle journalism
Game critics	Art and culture critics, including film, music, and television critics	Cultural criticism

are substantial connections among them owing to their overlapping and rapidly expanding spheres of coverage. In chapter 4, we argue that this overlap is partly the result of a large pool of freelancers, who submit pieces to a variety of organizations and are therefore less bound by institutional rules and expectations.

The first group of writers engaging in game journalism are *institutional journalists*, who see journalism as their main profession and who work for incumbent news organizations and legacy institutions (e.g., the *Wall Street Journal* or the *New Yorker*) or emerging news platforms (e.g., *Vox* or *Politico*). This category consists either of writers who consider games to be their "beat"—their main area of expertise—or those who have a broader editorial mandate, be it technology, arts, or entertainment. Institutional journalists are typically the most active in performing boundary work because they are subject to an existing set of normative expectations. Whereas game reviewers, critics, and developers rarely talk about a shared set of ethics or occupational norms, institutional journalists tend to constantly understand their own work through a range of ideal-type standards, or "occupational ideology."[23] These standards include such slippery notions as objectivity, allegiance to their audience, and fairness. For example, most institutional journalists abide by a clear set of ethics, often codified in an outlet's editorial guidelines, and operate with a degree of removal from the industries they cover.

Conversely, a great many game journalists tend to be associated more with various forms of either "lifestyle journalism" (e.g., travel or technology journalism), or "cultural criticism" (e.g., music, film, or television journalism) than with institutional reportage.[24] The second and third categories of authors are therefore *game reviewers* and *game critics*, two categories of writers who predominantly focus directly on games.[25] The distinction between this set of journalistic practices—reviewers and critics—is subtle and fleshed out by the game scholar and critic Ian Bogost, who argues that a reviewer "speaks from a position of investment," and a critic "speaks from a position of remove."[26] That is, game reviewers tend to stay very close to their object, engaging in

functional overviews "full of technical details and thor-
ough testing and final, definitive scores delivered on
improbably precise numerical scales."[27] Reviewers predominantly work for organizations dedicated to game
coverage, such as magazines (e.g., *Edge*, *Game Informer*)
or online outlets (e.g., *IGN*, *Kotaku*, *Polygon*). In past academic works, game reviewers have been categorized as
the "specialist" or the "enthusiast press," deeply immersed
in game fandom, discussing games as peers but not
equals, and drawing on intimate knowledge of past
games and events.[28]

It is because of the more explicit—and arguably
stricter—occupational ideology of institutional journalists that reviewers tend to actively resist the "journalist" label. For instance, Patrick Prax and Alejandro
Soler found that game reviewers would refer to their
colleagues as "journalists" while "not claiming this title
and the responsibility that comes with it" for themselves.[29] As such, journalism scholars understand them
as "lifestyle journalists," whose practices are similar to
"other forms of journalism outside the mainstream,"
such as travel, fashion, and food journalism.[30] Lifestyle
journalists, and thus reviewers, have a "strong market-
orientation" because they explicitly consider their
audience as consumers to whom they offer "practical
advice" in a way that is meant to be entertaining.[31]

The close relationship that game reviewers share with
the industry and their particular objects of interest dis-
tinguishes them from critics and journalists. The former
tend to establish their roles as mediators through an

intimate industry relationship, leading them to act as both arbiter and promoter of content, whereas institutional journalists and game critics take a more rigorous stance in separating themselves from the subjects and industries they cover. If reviewers are the ultimate fans or insiders, then game critics are outsiders, and purposely so. Like reviewers, game critics may write for dedicated game or institutional outlets, just as Paumgarten did in the *New Yorker*. For Bogost, himself a critic par excellence, "good criticism" answers the question "What is even going on here?"[32] Critics can be scholars, students, or autodidacts who often start out reviewing games; as their careers progress, they move on to create more critical distance and broaden their purview. As such, game critics have a tendency to ask questions that fans and industry insiders deem "difficult" or "political," meaning that they clash with the general culture of positivity, anticipation, and approval that is at the heart of game fandom.[33] For a critic to write a game preview—an indepth, descriptive analysis of an impending release—would not be an obvious choice; for reviewers, it is one of their main staples. That said, there is a fine line between being critical of a game's technical features—pointing to a low framerate, for instance—and challenging the status quo. The former you will see mentioned in enthusiast press game reviews; the latter is something that critics (should) do by alluding to broader questions of social justice, (media) history, or precarious labor practices among developers. If game reviewers practice a form of lifestyle journalism, game critics come much closer to "cultural journalism," which is "specialized in reporting about arts and culture and preoccupied with maintaining a distinct professional identity."[34] In this sense, they are more aligned with the occupational ideology of institutional journalists.

To some, our typology may seem artificial, or even useless. All three groups are simply game journalists (or writers), who should "objectively" review games.[35] For others, these categories are soon to be extinct; the popularity of the hyperindividualistic approach to discussing games taken by streamers such as Markiplier, Fernanfloo, and Freyline further blurs the boundaries between reviewers and critics and pushes traditional journalism's institutional norms to their breaking point.[36] Regardless, we tease out these distinctions because the blurring of these three types represents daily personal battles for game journalists of any stripe. Instead of arbitrarily delimiting content (e.g., an essay, a review, or a "hard" news article), we focus on *how* games are depicted and by *whom*, thereby emphasizing how journalists engage in boundary work, or the constant negotiation of their implied mandate, as well as the ideological and gatekeeping functions inherent to their profession.

The Mainstreaming of Games

Apart from discussing the everyday work and self-perceptions of practitioners, we are interested in how they contribute to the broader acceptance and under-standing of games. As more and more journalists and outlets incorporate games into their beat, we have wit-nessed a qualitative change in articles' structure, tone, and subject matter. These changes in coverage are largely prompted by the undeniable quantitative shift in the authors' implied audience (i.e., those who play or watch others play), which has grown bigger and contin-ues to become more and more diverse. Bigger, however, does not necessarily infer mainstream. So, what does it mean when we invoke the "mainstreaming" label? Scholarly definitions of what constitutes "the main-stream media," mainstream coverage, or mainstream media practices tend to be one-dimensional, using notions such as "commercially dominant" or "corpo-rate," thereby assuming broad commercial and public appeal to a wide audience.[37] For us, these definitions are too narrow. We are wary of commercial viability as the sole marker of success. Many profitable media forms and genres are hardly considered to be mainstream in terms of their visibility—comic books and pornography immediately come to mind.

More so, digital play is too meaningful to be measured solely by how well it performs in the market. Other quantitative indicators, such as the number of down-loads or players, are also too limiting as benchmarks; mainstream acceptance would mean not mass appeal but broad appeal—popularity among not merely one large homogenous group (e.g., young people) but rather widespread adoption across regions and intersectional categories (i.e., gender, ethnicity, class, sexuality, ability, age, etc.). Last, rather than using binary terms—games are either mainstream or not—we aim to identify a less static set of markers. Because of these limitations, we seek a set of variables—heuristics, if you will—against which we can track whether games are becoming more (or less) mainstream.

The media scholar Jason Toynbee provides a helpful definition based on his historical study of popular music: "the mainstream brings together large numbers of people from diverse social groups in common affiliation to a musical style."[38] He notes that mainstreaming should be considered "an ambivalent social process" that oscillates between broader acceptance and acknowledgment of differences from nonmainstream styles.[39] For our purposes, the strength of Toynbee's analysis—its focus on music—is also its weakness. Mainstreaming does have a quantitative dimension ("large numbers of people") and it is an ambivalent process, not unlike the ambiguity observed by Kirkpatrick. Importantly, Toynbee points to acceptance ("common affiliation") of musical styles as a prerequisite to being mainstream; jazz was a mainstream music style by the 1930s, and rock by the 1960s.

Yet, this argument implies the broader acceptance of listening to music as a cultural practice in and of itself. It is telling that Toynbee talks about certain musical *styles* being mainstream but not so much about the act of listening to music. Making music and publicly or privately listening to music is typically not considered deviant, let alone addictive. Similarly, although "cult movies" are understood to be alternatives to mainstream, commercial cinema, the practice of watching Hollywood movies became a mainstream pastime as early as the 1960s.[40] This is to say that the notion of "the mainstream" in media scholarship is always relative and implies *intra-media* popularity among genres, publishers, or auteurs. In this case, boundaries are drawn by scholars and industry actors among mainstream movies, songs, comics, or games versus alternative or independently created ("indie") content.[41]

In this book we take an *inter-media* perspective, contending that games as a media form and gameplay as a practice have not been mainstream since they reached commercial success in the 1980s. Rather than using economic impact as the only metric of acceptance, we posit that for games to be considered a mainstream cultural practice, they require access (ubiquity), a shared understanding (literacy), and a modicum of acceptance (legitimacy). As long as one of these is lacking, we do not consider games to be "mainstream." Let us examine these three variables and how they relate to each other.

The *Fortnite* article at the start of this introduction serves as an example of games becoming more ubiquitous. Similarly, because of widespread access to mobile phones and the burgeoning app economy, billions of users have access to digital games, which points to their greater cultural visibility. Games have moved from a niche—or, as we will discuss in the next chapter, "subcultural"—interest toward more general diffusion and adoption. At the same time, however, the *Fortnite* example also demonstrates the limits of considering ubiquity as the sole marker of mainstreaming. Access does not equal understanding.

Ludic literacy—the embodied comprehension of a game's procedural logic (an understanding of its rules and mechanics) and its operation (which buttons to push or how to boot up a game in the first place)—is far from universal.[42] An additional complicating factor is the medium's "cultural inaccessibility," described by the game scholar and critic Emma Vossen as "various cultural barriers that either deliberately or unconsciously exclude people" and may potentially cause them to feel unwelcome and unsafe "because of their identities."[43] As we will see, the high literacy requirements in addition to the rampant, ongoing gatekeeping by insiders are frustrating to newcomers who want to learn how to play, let alone those who aim to engage in any form of game critique.

This second prerequisite of having a shared understanding presents a wealth of challenges to critics. Recall Paumgarten's rhetorical question: "Shall I explain the game?" His query underscores that the ruleset for every single game is unique, often complex, and contingent. Conversely, the rules for listening to almost any rock song are rather straightforward, singular, relatively set, and uniform. The genre is "extremely coherent" as a musical style; songs often share a 4/4 time signature as well as similar themes, melodies, and patterns.[44] Games, on the other hand, typically merit video tutorials to explain each unique set of rules. Moreover, to be able to play an advanced game like *Fortnite*, one also needs to have some rudimentary understanding of the game platform. When playing on a PC, for example, a player moves their mouse to point at an enemy and shoots by clicking a mouse button. But to arrive at that point, one must first install the game and ideally be somewhat familiar with the genre traits of "shooter" games. Thus, digital games may be economically vibrant, played more than ever before in their history, and within the purview of major news outlets, but the medium's inherent complexities present an enduring limitation to it becoming a mainstream, widely understood activity in the vein of listening to music or reading a novel.

Third, meeting the thresholds of ubiquity and universal comprehension does not necessarily guarantee cultural legitimacy. For example, watching television has become a pervasive practice that does not require instructions and has risen on the cultural ladder to the rung of a respectable pastime. But television's cultural acceptance is a fairly recent phenomenon. It was only in the 1970s and 1980s when "highbrow publications began to treat upscale television shows in terms once reserved for more established arts."[45] To be fair, games may be nearing a similar inflection point in some parts of the world. In South Korea, for instance, games and competitive play hold cultural standing similar to that of physical sports in North America.[46] Likewise, across the globe we are increasingly seeing some cultural markers being met: games have museums dedicated to them (such as the Strong Museum of Play in Rochester, New York) and are integrated into university curricula. Reputable news outlets also cover games, and even take them seriously at times. Still, we can only conclude that digital play continues to encounter rampant antagonism, bewilderment, and ambivalence. Here we see marked differences compared to other cultural forms. Popular musical taste is negotiated and must be constructed, Toynbee reminds us, but this happens on the level of styles, not music as a whole. Conversely, *every* game genre has its detractors. Politicians abhor violent video games, whereas gamers, critics, and journalists seem to look down on casual games. Many if not all of us routinely partake in the vilification of digital play as if to say: we can play, but whatever we do, we cannot take it *too* seriously.

These negative outbursts come to the fore in the long-running debate over whether games are art. Detractors argue that they are not and cannot be art because they are products—nonlinear, frivolous forms of commodified entertainment aimed at children.[47] As a result, numerous cultural critics find game journalism in any form to be a preposterous notion.[48] Suffice to say, we feel otherwise. For us, mainstreaming is not necessarily a qualitative label; it does not mean elitist or progressive, nor populist or conservative. Instead, we theorize it as a medium-specific indicator of ubiquity, comprehension, *and* normalization. This approach ties into the crucial "so what?" question underlying our argument: What are the political stakes of mainstreaming?

The short answer: because play matters.[49] We consider play to be meaningful and that increased ludic literacy—a broader understanding of digital play—allows for more productive critiques that should result in more meaningful games that provide an ever-wider array of experiences and cater to more diverse audiences. To achieve this admittedly aspirational goal, game journalism has a vital role to play. By virtue of their coverage, game journalists increase visibility and comprehension and, in doing so, legitimize play in the process.

The Rules of the Road

Before diving into the historical and institutional context that frustrated the process of mainstreaming for decades, here is a brief note on our goals, scope, sources, and methods. This book is meant to be provocative but not polemic, and signals an effort to make a concise argument on the mainstreaming of games vis-à-vis game journalism.[50] Therefore, we have set some limitations, one of which is geographical. We have limited our purview mainly to the United States and sparingly include a handful of European and English-speaking countries and outlets for two main reasons. First, the short span of this book means that we are unable to provide a comparative case—for example, Czech or Finnish game journalism. Second, we faced some practical challenges, such as lacking the necessary cultural background and language skills to expand our geographical scope. That said, we are acutely aware of scholarship on the regional variations in newsroom cultures, the role of public broadcasting systems (or lack thereof), and many other determinants that impact local instances of news production and consumption.[51]

Because of our regional focus on the United States, many of our observations, conclusions, and proposed solutions may not be universally applicable. We return to this issue in the book's conclusion by reflecting on what we can take away from studying English-speaking game journalists and US instances of game journalism. Ultimately, we do hope that our work inspires similar regional studies of both game journalism and mainstreaming. We are not currently aware of such studies other than the ones we cited, or they exist in languages we unfortunately do not speak.

For academically inclined readers, our argument is situated in the broader fields of media and journalism studies. We consider games to be different from other media forms, but certainly not special. For those less familiar with game research, throughout the book we will also draw from a significant body of scholarship considered game studies. Such work tends to focus on the effects of games on users or broader culture. Research on the game industry is far less common than one might expect, and research on game journalism, broadly conceived, is so rare that "journalism" and "criticism" are not mentioned once in review articles surveying the state of the field.[52] Certainly, there is a small body of empirical work featuring the voices of game journalists that has proven invaluable for this project.[53] Even so, we decided to conduct twenty additional semistructured interviews with game journalists roughly between 2017 and 2020 to fill the gaps in past work and get a better sense of how practitioners perform boundary work, how they grapple with game culture's persistent ambivalence, and, most of all, how they conceive of mainstreaming.[54]

Last, we feel it is pertinent to briefly introduce ourselves. Who are "we?" David is a Professor of Media Studies at the University of Toronto and had a second career as a game journalist in the Netherlands for over a decade (2006–2016). He wrote over one hundred columns, feature articles, and essays for leading Dutch daily newspapers, game magazines, and blogs. Much of this book is informed by his experiences dealing with public relations teams, visiting game studios, going to press junkets, covering events, and so on. Maxwell is a Professor of Media Studies and Game Studies at the University of Oregon. His research explores the intersections of games, play, interactive and immersive media, and journalism, where he has focused both on how newsmakers cover these topics and on how they incorporate them into their own work and practice. As we fit the stereotype of prototypical gamers (i.e., we are both white dudes), we want to recognize that we enjoyed ready access to many key employees, events, games, and places, both virtual and physical to which others may not be privy. Throughout this book we want to leverage these unique insights and opportunities to tell a story about the mainstreaming of game journalism.

Additionally, introducing ourselves offers an occasion to be explicit about our politics. Over the last few decades, journalists, critics, and academics have been under attack—ranging from mild verbal abuse to serious assault—for their journalistic work, advocacy efforts, or affiliation with research associations.[55] It is worth emphasizing that those facing such attacks are predominantly women, people of color, LGBTQ+, and other members of marginalized groups.[56] Even though these attempts are ultimately self-defeating, they have had—and still have—a chilling effect. For example, the already small number of high-profile women engaging in various forms of game journalism started to dwindle in the mid-2010s, after reactionary sexism from Gamergate (discussed later) left them open to incessant attacks that were not merely symbolic but had significant real-life consequences.[57] Sadly, they also prove the point made by many of our colleagues about the relatively small but toxic game and fan communities.[58] In more ways than one, bad-faith actors—from anonymous trolls to visible haters—have claimed ownership over what qualifies as "good" game journalism, muddying the waters and thereby obfuscating issues that deserve scholarly and societal attention. This book is a modest, good-faith attempt to make the conversation about game journalism slightly less cloudy.

2

Moving Away from the Mainstream

In the spring of 2018, the release of the first footage from the blockbuster game *Battlefield V* made quite a splash. Established in 2002 by the game studio EA DICE, the *Battlefield* series allows players to take on the role of a soldier in wars past, present, and future. The "official reveal trailer" released on YouTube (figure 2.1) offered fans and critics a first chance to see what the developers had been up to since the release of *Battlefield 1* in 2016.[1] The beginning of the clip had no taglines, or any text for that matter. Instead, it opened with a female soldier jumping off a tank, running into a house, and shooting the first moving person. Within seconds, she is killed in turn, and what follows is pure pandemonium. Set in World War II, we see an open, brightly lit battlefield where a chaotic firefight ensues; bridges collapse, a jeep falls from the sky and flattens a soldier, and a German V-1 flying bomb explodes in front of the camera. Much of the trailer contains surprisingly photorealistic visuals and, by all accounts, exhibits a massive feat of software engineering. The collective attention of fans, however, wandered elsewhere.

Figure 2.1
Battlefield V's release trailer on YouTube with over 16 million views as of late 2022. Source: Battlefield YouTube channel, "Battlefield 5 Official Reveal Trailer," uploaded May 23, 2018, https://youtu.be/fb1 MR85XFOc.

In less than two weeks after its release, the clip attracted over ten million views, 200,000 comments, and dozens of reaction videos critiquing the game's direction, each with hundreds of thousands of views and comments of their own. Those who responded directly to the original trailer were unhappy, to put it mildly. The inclusion of a female protagonist upset lots of fans. One commenter echoed the sentiments of many when they argued that "this is what happens when a company tries to force a political ideology through players' throat[s], instead [of] just making a good game." Others implied that a "good" World War II game would not include women in a fighting role because *that* would be "historically inaccurate:" "So progressive. I forgot that women with mechanical arms won WW2, thanks for reminding me. #Failure."

What to make of these emotions that oscillated between anger and betrayal? Why should one care about fans who felt that the developer abandoned "historical accuracy" in favor of "political correctness?" For outsiders such as parents, critics, and institutional journalists, these kinds of statements are so preposterous it is hard to take them seriously. This toxic cocktail of reactionary conservatism and outright misogyny among fans makes it apparent that best-selling games are not part of mainstream culture. For insiders who are familiar with this style of war game, the blatant hypocrisy of invoking historical accuracy in a genre known for its revisionist history—and incredibly limited portrayal of mechanized warfare's horrific consequences—is equally disheartening.[2] What self-respecting institutional journalistic organization would find this instance of adolescent indignation newsworthy?

Regardless, *Battlefield V* was not a small release, nor were these toxic conversations reserved for the dark corners of the internet. Instead, they represented *Battlefield*'s loyal, vocal, and financially lucrative consumer base. This episode is therefore relevant to our understanding of mainstreaming because these kinds of "technomasculine" conversations have been the rule, not the exception.[3] Analyzing contemporary game culture and its constitutive ambivalences inevitably brings us to the *subcultural* roots of *core* game culture. "Subcultural," as argued by Mikolaj Dymek, refers to the understanding of games as a niche medium "differentiated from the majority culture."[4] Likewise, core gamers (as opposed to casual or "noncore") represent the most dedicated parts of a community for whom being a *gamer* is a cultural identity.[5] As succinctly put by Emma Vossen: "While all players are gamers, not all players are Gamers."[6] Therefore, when using the label of "gamer" in this book, we refer to those players who embraced this inherently exclusionary subject position. To be clear, we are not implying that *all* gamers are misogynists, or that *all* gamers act in bad faith when engaging in heated online debates. Rather, we simply observe that for decades gamers have inhabited virtual worlds largely impenetrable to outsiders, thereby preventing greater ubiquity and literacy and ultimately thwarting cultural legitimacy—as exemplified by the *Battlefield V* trailer reactions.

In this chapter, we argue that games have become more subcultural over the years, a development perpetuated by a triad of gamers, game journalists, and the game industry. We start off by providing a brief history of gaming's subcultural era. Then, we reflect on the role of the enthusiast press during this time, after which we survey the historical rise of the core game industry and its responsibility in shaping the subcultural imaginary of games. We argue that together with critics, the industry largely sets the norms for what it has meant, and continues to mean, to be a "real" gamer playing "real" games.[7] We close the chapter by discussing how institutional journalists writing for newspapers and magazines have attempted to make sense of games, gamers, and the industry. Faced with strife and uncertainty, journalists have wobbled between aspirational coverage framing games as exciting novelties and falling back on deep-seated moral panics such as addiction, displacement, and the notion that games are inherently infantile. For decades, journalists have reified games and gamers' subcultural—and ultimately extremist—tendencies, thereby thwarting the mainstreaming of the medium.

Throughout this chapter, we will theorize this decades-long historical development of self-inflicted alienation through the lens of capital: economic capital (money) and forms of game capital (expert knowledge and status). On the one hand, developing and publishing blockbuster games has been—and remains—a risky business proposition that requires massive economic investment to pull off.[8] Hundreds of developers in Sweden and around the world crafted and honed *Battlefield V* until the moment it was released at the cost of tens of millions of dollars. Additionally, players and journalists require some serious ludic literacy to critique *Battlefield V*'s trailer. Thus, beyond the game's price tag, players must know about *Battlefield*'s franchise history, genre conventions, and game discourse, which game scholar

Mia Consalvo has collectively theorized as "game capital."[9] We demonstrate that the capital requirements to productively engage with game culture have only increased over time.

Shaping a Subculture

After switching from analog to digital, a rough periodization of the evolution of the game industry would be: arcade, subcultural, casual, and postcasual. Each period overlaps, and technologies and practices dominant in earlier periods never disappear completely; for instance, analog games, or board and card games, are currently going through an extended revival of their own. Here, we focus on the early part of this history—the arcade and subcultural eras—when game culture failed to gain mainstream status.

Inspired by Graeme Kirkpatrick's scholarship, we want to emphasize that this historical trajectory should not be considered natural, inevitable, or predetermined.[10] Unlike today's bracketed understanding of digital play, being playful is not inherently exclusionary: "Play is something that all humans do and it has been present in all cultures."[11] Industrial capitalism, however, did prompt a change in the perception of play. For centuries, it operated largely outside the confines of commodity culture; nobody owns the rules or intellectual property of analog games such as go, chess, poker, or spades. In North America, the rise of mass consumer culture and semipublic places featuring analog play changed this dynamic, from penny arcades and family fun centers to the introduction of video game arcades in the early 1970s. Coin-operated game machines like *Pong* (1972) and *Pac-Man* (1980) introduced millions of North Americans to a new form of digital play and laid the foundation for a multibillion-dollar industry. Unlike most contemporary forms of play, however, playing in arcades was a *public* consumer practice, which goes to show the crucial role of industry in setting the socio-cultural and economic parameters of player behavior, game formats, and business models.[12]

Many of contemporary game culture's constitutive ambivalences mentioned in the previous chapter can be traced back to these formative decades. In the 1970s United States, the introduction of video games to coin-op arcades paralleled the introduction of dedicated home game consoles. At this point, their meaning as technological novelties, the identities of their players, and their associated business models were hardly set in stone. Science and technology studies scholars remind us that technological innovations go through a phase of "interpretive flexibility" and are subsequently socially shaped.[13] For example, dedicated home consoles—such as the 1977 Atari Video Computer System (VCS)— emerged along with the social and technological evo-lution of the television set.[14] Thus, their introduction built on historical traces of cultural anxiety and friction, as watching excessive amounts of television in the 1960s and 1970s was considered wasteful, disreputable, and a passive experience.[15]

It took a decade of negotiations over meanings and values among industry professionals, players, politicians, institutional journalists, and cultural critics for games to arrive at their subcultural position. Initially, dedicated console manufacturers did cast a wide net as demonstrated by print advertising that depicted families playing together in front of their TV sets. Yet, this changed in the late 1970s when the first megahits—in particular, the Atari VCS version of *Space Invaders* (1980) —redirected the industry's course. Rather than engage in the discursive battle for cultural legitimacy, industry leaders moved away from the mainstream and advertised heavily to a narrower demographic. Video game technology that initially brought families together morphed into escapist fare for boys.[16] Starting in the late 1970s, dedicated game consoles began to be associated with youthful, masculine, and middle-class players.[17]

No history of the subcultural era would be complete without mentioning the infamous gaming console industry crash that unfolded over the course of 1983 to 1985 in North America. A glut of low-quality titles for consoles such as the Atari VCS made many players reconsider their investments in time and money. To benefit from this lull in demand, the Japanese console manufacturer Nintendo entered the US market and introduced the Nintendo Entertainment System (NES) just before the 1985 holiday season. In his canonical study *Diffusion of Innovations*, communication theorist Everett Rogers explains how Nintendo regained consumer confidence and turned the NES into a bestseller.[18] For instance, Nintendo aimed its advertising at children, who reportedly begged their parents for the new machine. To further broaden the device's appeal, Nintendo's marketing department positioned the NES as a toy rather than a computer. This repositioning not only improved the console's reputation as a family-friendly device but also established Nintendo as being invested in players' game literacy. The company opened call centers to help consumers troubleshoot problems and began publishing a magazine, *Nintendo Power*, which offered tips and tricks for players.[19] Although the company took a different approach from its competitors, whether Nintendo's efforts have contributed to the mainstreaming of games in the long run is still up for debate. Rogers observed that over the course of 1986, "young boys became addicted to the Nintendo games, particularly those featuring Mario the plumber."[20] As we will see later in this chapter, the NES may have rekindled a broken industry, but Nintendo's focus on those boys, coupled with the way *Nintendo Power* brought in players, did not alter gaming's subcultural spiral as the company failed to broaden beyond the console's implied adolescent male audience.

The First Decades of the Enthusiast Press

During the subcultural era, as the industry increasingly catered to a niche cohort, dedicated game publications emerged "to cash in on the craze for video games by selling magazines and books to mostly young male video game enthusiasts."[21] As Kirkpatrick observes, it is at this very moment that game magazines helped create the conditions for digital play to "become sexist" and thus to occupy and subsequently normalize its subcultural position.[22] Before we address the everyday (work) life of game journalists in the next chapter, let us provide historical context on how game magazine culture evolved during the 1980s and 1990s.

If, as the saying goes, journalists write the first draft of history, what would the first draft of game history look like through the eyes of game critics and reviewers? When we surveyed game and journalism studies, research into this question is conspicuously absent. Although scholars frequently seek out game magazines as source material for their analyses, historical accounts of the industry rarely offer insight into the work and position of critics and reviewers.[23]

Since an in-depth analysis of decades of US game magazine culture lies outside of the scope of this book, we turn to those partial views and historical snippets. For example, *Digital Play: The Interaction of Culture, Technology, and Marketing*—Stephen Kline and colleagues' influential scholarly review of the game industry's history

—only mentions game magazines in passing through a discussion of *Nintendo Power*.[24] Founded in 1988 by a member of Nintendo of America's marketing team, the periodical (figure 2.2) became one of the best-selling game magazines in the United States.[25] With Nintendo as its financier, the outlet was the domain of the game reviewer rather than the game critic. One would be hard pressed to find investigations or essays that "aim to question, contest" and "evaluate" among its pages.[26] Instead, the magazine focused on formulaic previews and reviews, which have obvious evaluative aims: to find out "whether something is good or bad in its category," or to discover a game's "possible worth or value."[27] Crucially, *Nintendo Power* played an important role in terms of boosting game literacy, one of our three conditions to mainstreaming. The magazine offered tips, tricks, guides, and cheat codes—key pieces of "game capital"—as well as answers to reader-submitted questions.[28]

Subscribers paid fifteen dollars per year (by the 1990s) for the privilege to read what amounted to sanctioned propaganda.[29] Billing itself as "The Source for NES Players Straight from the Pros," the publication calcified the relationship between game reviewers, the industry, and fans.[30] Whereas maintaining a strict boundary between editorial content and marketing material may be sacrosanct for institutional journalists, any such divide was obviously absent in Nintendo's magazine. As such, *Nintendo Power* became a catalyst for the enthusiast press by

Figure 2.2
A page from *Nintendo Power*. Source: Brian Hoss, "R.I.P. Nintendo Power," *The Bonus View* (blog), August 23, 2012, https://www.highdef digest.com/blog/nintendo-power-canceled/.

providing a template of what a game magazine could look like: "[Its] popularity helped to establish a format for game content and news—glossy spreads and high-profile, in-depth coverage of forthcoming games, very similar to the content found in video game magazines and Web sites today."[31] Despite its fame and didactic efforts, the magazine's contributions toward main-streaming belied its squandered potential for broad market appeal. *Nintendo Power* was purposely targeted at the predictable demographic of young male consumers. Its authors were largely male, players presented in the magazine were overwhelmingly male, and female characters were sexualized.[32] Any emancipatory movements and efforts, therefore, were unable to combat these structural inequities and failed to gain traction in its influential pages and other similar publications.

One of the most comprehensive studies of early instances of game journalism outside of North America has been conducted by Graeme Kirkpatrick, whom we introduced in the previous chapter. His books provide an in-depth look at how UK game magazines discursively shaped concepts, tastes, and dispositions from the early 1980s to the mid-1990s.[33] Initially, players were hailed as exactly that—players rather than gamers. There was no predetermined way to talk about the medium, to evaluate products, or to assume who its audience could (or should) be. Like the game reviews, articles, and letters to the editor that would appear in *Nintendo Power*, the authors of 1980s British game magazines slowly but steadily started to deploy rhetorical strategies that were increasingly exclusionary to women, older players, and even such enthusiasts as computer tinkerers and hobbyists. "Good" games went from typically describing well-programmed software to instead referring to content that required adequate "gameplay." This amorphous concept could only be understood by a "real" gamer, which had become a fixed, gendered identity. "Computer games did not inherit their masculine symbolism from anywhere else: it was produced as part of the process whereby digital gaming established itself as a cultural practice in the second half of the 1980s."[34] That is to say, digital play came into its own, discursively, technologically, and economically, through the process of othering, and game reviewers played a vital role in doing so.

Toward New Games Journalism

US game magazines evolved in parallel to their UK counterparts. The independently published *Electronic Gaming Monthly* (*EGM*) was founded around the same time as *Nintendo Power*, but its autonomy should be taken with a grain of salt. As Dominic Arsenault argues, it was hard for "editors to do anything more than relay, almost verbatim, the inflected descriptions they received from hardware manufacturers."[35] Although it was not solely dedicated to one platform, the magazine featured article types like those found in *Nintendo Power*: reader letters, strategy sections, cheats and tricks, and the magazine's bread-and-butter, previews and reviews. By following these formats—and in line with Kirkpatrick's analysis—*EGM* "taught players how to play generally, what to expect from a game, and how to evaluate games."[36] This is something scholars studying the subcultural era widely agree on: enthusiast magazines set and shaped expectations on how to play well, how to talk about games, what counted as game journalism, what to value in a game, and the implied audience for both hardware and software. After *EGM*, many new magazines—*GamePro* (1989), *Game Informer* (1991), *PC Gamer* (1993), and *Edge* (1993)—continued in this mold, with some titles attracting hundreds of thousands of subscribers. Decades later, a handful of magazines sustain an immense subscriber base; with over 2 million subscribers, *Game Informer*—published monthly by the retail chain GameStop—ranks in the global top 5 of magazine circulation.

Our emphasis on early US game magazine culture and how it shaped the occupational and discursive practices of the enthusiast press stems from how it fostered important frames and tropes; magazine genre formats emerged and writers started to cater to a clearly targeted demographic. By contrast, the World Wide Web and affordable digital publishing tools theoretically could have changed the subcultural trajectory of game coverage. Anyone with a keyboard and internet access was suddenly able to challenge the status quo and publish industry-related information. They could also write critical essays to either legitimize games as an art form or promote a new shared vocabulary with a decidedly non-subcultural flavor. Yet this possibility did not materialize. The diffusion of "new media" technologies is often associated with utopian ideals, such as democratization of readers and publishers. This view, however, ignores the lure of commodity culture, entrenched occupational ideologies among reviewers and critics, and game journalists' need for access to industry-supplied game capital.

In the 1990s, many US households gained internet access; technologically literate gamers were among its earliest adopters. There are few scholarly investigations of the switch from magazine publishing to online distribution in gaming. Websites from the 1990s included *Game Zero*, which "first offered video game related content that served as a supplement for print magazines."[37] Over time, rather than remediating magazines, online-exclusive outfits such as *IGN* (1996) and *GameSpot* (1996), and later *Kotaku* (2004) and *Giant Bomb* (2008), became key US-based venues for video game journalism. On the heels of an industry that showed no sign of economic decline, the business of game journalism became subject to rapid consolidation. Attracted by its millions of monthly visitors, News Corporation bought *IGN* in 2005 for $650 million, only to sell it to publisher Ziff Davis in 2013. Similar websites were either acquired by transnational media corporations (e.g., *GameSpot*'s purchase by *CNET*), merged with other outfits (e.g., *Joystiq* being absorbed by *Engadget*), or shut down (e.g., *1up*, *UGO*, and *GameSpy*). *IGN* proved to be particularly resilient and is still going strong with 200+ employees, of which 100 are editors. Its impressive collection of 30+ regional editions draw an international audience of nearly 300 million.

In the mid-2000s, alongside the popularization of game websites, a vast online ecosystem started to proliferate that was as creatively rich as it was prolific. This dizzying array of personal game sites, blogs, wikis, and message boards provided the means for players to access the latest news, seek information and validation, and create community. The line between fans and the enthusiast press, and between game reviewers and critics, blurred even further. As Dan Golding argues, "People created semi-academic tracts, magazine-style feature articles, memoirs, beat-inspired poetry, and strident, manifesto-like sermons. By the end of the 2000s, critical videogame writing had gone well beyond 'review.'"[38]

This moment also marked an important attempt at a shift in style. Game journalist Kieron Gillen's manifesto "The New Games Journalism" is frequently singled out as encapsulating the desire to move away from the strict confines of game reviews as buyer's guides. His "new dogma" boils down to "1) The worth of gaming lies in the gamer not the game" and "2) Write travel journalism to Imaginary Places."[39] Instead of focusing on a game's aesthetics and technical prowess, journalists were encouraged to recount the highly individual experience of play. Although it never intended to steer all journalists in the same direction, Gillen's manifesto still received a fair amount of pushback at the time.

Sites to facilitate "ongoing conversations between developers, critics, educators and enthusiasts," such as *Critical Distance* (2009), or to engage in literary game criticism, such as *Kill Screen* (2010), emerged. These initiatives allowed for the important work of intellectualization: an attempt to pull the medium from the lower rungs of the cultural hierarchy and legitimize it. As valiant as these efforts were, democratizing the means of distribution resulted instead in further nichification, thwarting both the preservation of institutional memory and creation of shared vocabulary.[40] In the subsequent two decades of feverish debates over style, key concepts, tone, formats, content, and subjects, game journalists never seemed to reach any meaningful consensus,[41] nor did a coherent occupational identity emerge as they collectively continued to wrestle with their professional status.[42]

Perpetuating Upgrade Culture

As indicated by the popularity of *Nintendo Power*, *Game Informer*, and *IGN*, the enthusiast press evolved in discursive lockstep with the industry. Together they internalized what James Newman dubbed "the lure of the imminent," or the idea that there is an "irresistible sense of 'progress' and the new is always unproblematically 'better' than that which it replaces."[43] Similarly, in his in-depth study of the 1987 TurboGrafx-16 home console, Carl Therrien points to the press's focus on the platform's supposed technological superiority by drawing on warfare rhetoric.[44] Throughout the 1990s and far beyond, game magazines, blogs, and websites all continuously hyped the idea of hardware companies waging a "personified technological conflict of cosmic proportions," with victories meted out according to photorealism and graphical fidelity rather than exploring a game's accessibility or encouraging cultural ubiquity.[45]

From the 1980s to the early 2000s, the subcultural era "normalised a cultural imagination of the videogame as consumer software driven by innovations in processing power and graphical fidelity, an increasing amount of content and scale, and limited to a finite number of action-centric genres."[46] Atari and Nintendo, and later Sega, Sony, and Microsoft, became the poster children of this "perpetual-innovation economy," which is marked by short production cycles, constantly upgraded hardware and software, and the aggressive policing of intellectual property rights.[47] The moment a new console launches, manufacturers start the process of designing the next platform, which is then promised to be a significant improvement over the current cycle.

Each "generation" has a lifespan of roughly seven to ten years, introducing new controllers, more storage, faster chips, and of course, improved graphics for more "realistic" games.[48] Blockbusters, or AAA ("Triple-A") games, would become so-called killer apps or system sellers— games that drive consumer investment in new hardware. And invest they have: The global game industry's revenue numbers are on a seemingly never-ending upward trajectory. Players keep spending on hardware and software, prompting global game publishers and tech conglomerates to heavily invest in research, development, and marketing.

As a result of this cycle, games have become "constitutive of twenty-first-century global hypercapitalism" in which corporate ownership is highly concentrated and large publishers exert outsized control over what is developed and by whom.[49] Every new console cycle requires more economic capital from all involved, increasing risk aversion in turn. Hardware developers fund more research and development, software studios expand their teams, and game publishers require bigger marketing campaigns to presell their upcoming titles. Whereas in the age of the Atari VCS, a handful of developers could code an entire hit like *Pong* by themselves, a blockbuster game such as 2018's *Red Dead Redemption 2* requires tens of millions of dollars to develop via thousands of highly skilled workers, each of whom contributes a tiny part to designing an entire virtual world, its marketing campaign, and increasingly, its back-end services. New platforms and tools—mobile devices, affordable game engines, and cloud computing—may have lowered production budgets, but the cycle of pent-up supply and demand has yet to stop in the console segment.

Perpetual upgrade culture is not a top-down dictate by the industry but rather one that is sustained and even encouraged by gamers and game journalists alike. The pages of game magazines in the 1980s and '90s, and blogs and websites in the 2000s, were stacked with stories about unrealized potential in new games and to-be-released devices. Constant updates and the promise of something better just around the corner provided game journalists with endless amounts of copy. Reviewers adopted a rhetoric of anticipation rather than reflection;[50] less "Do we need this machine? How will it impact gameplay? How are these games made and what is their (imagined) audience?" and more "Which company made this marvelous new device? When will it be available? And, most importantly, who is 'winning' this hardware cycle?" These never-ending generational "battles" (Nintendo vs. Sega, Sony vs. Microsoft, etc.) provide a particularly useful frame for writers and publishers alike.[51]

The effect of perpetual update culture on the mainstreaming of games is therefore manifold. First, it increases the economic and game capital requirements of gamers. With every new franchise installment, a player typically faces more complex play, which in

turn means more investment in the franchise to understand its expanded lore, narrative, or mechanics. Second, upgrade culture is at the very root of the industry's
self-imposed creative conservatism. As Brendan Keogh
astutely observes, blockbuster production "aggressively
formalized"; for game publishers, the economic benefit to publish one more installment in a long-running
series far outweighs the risks of investing in original
intellectual property.[52] For decades, those players interested in games that went beyond these narrow cultural
and institutional boundaries essentially have been told
to look elsewhere.

If the enthusiast press has focused on teaching proper
gameplay and fueling the anticipatory drumbeat of
new technology, institutional journalists have marched
in a decidedly different direction. Catering to a much
broader audience—and one typically lacking in ludic
literacy, at that—institutional journalists contributed
to the further bifurcation of game culture by framing
games as innovative and educational technology, addictive toys, or, even worse, the devil's playthings.

Constructing Fun and Fear

Although the industry may have set expectations about
games through both advertising campaigns and their
decisions of what to publish, institutional news outlets
also recognized games' mass appeal and subsequently
covered them widely throughout the subcultural era.

This raises the question: Did institutional journalists contribute to the mainstreaming of games, or to their subcultural spiral? We argue the latter. Like the *Fortnite* "craze" in the *New Yorker*, the reportage of institutional journalists oscillates between hope and fear, between appreciation and bewilderment. Rather than promoting game literacy or normalizing play, they have contributed to enduring ambivalence about game culture.

As with the enthusiast press, there is remarkably little research on institutional game journalism—that is, coverage of games and game culture in national newspapers and news magazines—during the industry's formative decades. For example, sustained analyses of how US newspapers covered the rise of game consoles, or how institutional journalists and editors grappled with game culture, are rare. One notable exception is Dmitri Williams's study of US news coverage during the 1970–2000 period.[53] Finding a contradictory set of utopian and dystopian frames, he argues that games "passed through marked phases of vilification followed by partial redemption."[54] Initially, the media countered public fears of truancy and discussed physical skills required and the educational value of play. Later, utopian frames positioned games to be fun, social, and an important way to familiarize children with technology. Conversely, the fear of games as a new technology resonated with wider social concerns in the 1980s such as criminality and drug use, supporting the stereotype that playing games is a wasteful activity. Williams shows that an effect-based line of reasoning took hold in the United

States by the 1990s, portraying digital play as pathological and gamers as antisocial and potentially aggressive. Several flashpoints, most famously the Columbine High School shooting in 1999, cemented the latter frame of games as dangerous, even though there is no causal connection between gameplay and such tragedies.

A subsequent study of game coverage in the *New York Times*, one of the most respected newspapers in the United States, dovetails with both Williams's findings and Kirkpatrick's argument; game coverage in the publication has been dominated by a deep sense of ambivalence. In the 1980s and 1990s, the *Times* predominantly portrayed games as a "social threat," yet at the same time allowed space for counternarratives that extolled the medium's social benefits. In the 2000s, there was a marked shift in the *Times*'s coverage as articles began to "praise video games for their capacity to provide players with powerful social experiences."[55] Crucially, such articles appeared in the paper's Arts section, suggesting that games had finally moved into the purview of cultural critics, who reflected on games' artistic merits.

By conscripting game journalism into the realm of arts criticism, a different bifurcation emerged—one centered around cultural legitimacy. Distinctions emerged between high culture and low culture, between "prestige" games and regular run-of-the-mill titles.[56] Institutional journalists seem to have a clear sense of which games are worthy of coverage and attention: titles such as *Fortnite, Grand Theft Auto V, BioShock,* and *Pokémon Go*

claim the spotlight because of their economic impact or
artistic value, leaving out thousands of other titles. As
a result of new audiences, genres, and game platforms,
"there has been growing uncertainty, manifesting alter-
nately as ambivalence and sharp disagreement, about
what precisely, at this time of rapid mutation and prolif-
eration of the form, constitutes the object of inquiry."[57]
Games such as *Hay Day*, *Game of War*, the latest *League
of Legends* update, or any of the dozens of social casino
apps (e.g., *Slotomania Casino* or *Big Fish Casino*) are
apparently part of a different, less newsworthy category. Among these titles, noncore games in particular
are rarely deemed worthy of criticism. As one institutional game journalist writing for a quality newspaper
once told us when asked about his decision not to write
about the then-popular social network game *FarmVille*,
"We do not review romance novels, either." Although
this remark was made seemingly off the cuff, it speaks to
casual games' subcultural and gendered status. Casual
games are not considered "real games."[58] This is partially
influenced by the perception that games such as *Farm-
Ville* are associated with a "feminine leisure style."[59]

For myriad reasons, which we will discuss more in
depth in the following chapters, national US newspapers and magazines have been reluctant to structurally
invest in dedicated game editors. In an overview for
The Ringer, Ben Lindbergh describes the ways in which
the *New York Times* and the *Wall Street Journal* have
thus far resisted accepting games in the pantheon of

arts criticism that includes theater, film, and music.[60] Lindbergh notes that the tension between catering to "mainstream" newspaper audiences versus those who are more game literate is a key issue in game journalism gaining mainstream status: "The challenge is providing a blend of accessibility and credibility." In chapters 4 and 5, we will draw on conversations with newspaper and magazine reporters to dig deeper into contemporary modes of national newspaper coverage and discuss the many challenges game journalists face when attempting to cater to broader audiences.

Playing the Boundary Police

To better understand the past, present, and potential future of digital play, imagine the field as a world of extremes permeated by a deep sense of doubt. From our bird's-eye overview of the history of the enthusiast press, the industry, and institutional journalism, we observed that all involved erected barriers and demarcated boundaries to police who is "in" and who is "out." Three pivotal barriers ultimately hinder the mainstreaming of games. First, there is a widespread literacy barrier. No one reporter will ever comprehend such a heterogeneous industry that includes simple apps, sprawling virtual worlds, and intricate franchises with histories that span decades. There are numerous systemic inequalities that make it incredibly hard, if not impossible, for many individuals to access these heavily curated communities and "level up" within them.[61] In fact, the exclusionary atmosphere constituting the subcultural era is sustained rather than resolved by the enthusiast press. Second, game journalists are forever unsure about digital play's legitimacy.[62] Reflecting on game coverage in the *New York Times*, Lindbergh notes that while the industry gets its fair share of attention, "the medium's demotion from the culture section reflects a curious, continuing lack of mainstream coverage, which persists 40 years after *Asteroids* despite steadily swelling revenue figures, ever-more-realistic visuals, increasingly sophisticated storytelling, and Ellen normalizing [*Fortnite* streamer] Ninja."[63]

Last, increased capital requirements hamper game technology's ubiquity. Critics, reviewers, editors, and publishers of journalism outlets—not to mention gamers, game developers, and publishers—collectively legitimized and normalized the continuous increase in money and game capital. To protect these investments, all parties have deployed a variety of risk-reduction strategies. For example, throughout the 1980s and 1990s, game console manufacturers and leading game publishers "deliberately" suppressed any form of informal or amateur game development.[64] Over the course of several console cycles, the game industry set the pace of innovation and shaped player discourse and expectations through mass-marketing campaigns. Rather than offering games that were cheaper, simpler, more accessible, and more adaptable, the industry purposely opted for a capital-intensive mode of development. Consequently, the increasing popularity of games has also made them more subcultural.

Game journalists, magazines, and websites have played a key role in normalizing, legitimizing, and marketing the industry's subcultural offerings. Critics and reviewers crafted and later maintained a culturally and historically specific idea of what digital games and play should look and feel like.[65] The resulting subculture repels "the majority of society" because it excludes "women, senior gamers and emerging markets."[66] Brendan Keogh makes a similar point as he argues that the subcultural era spawned a "conservative consumer culture of distribution platforms and enthusiast discourse that are used to videogames being a specific, homogenised practice."[67] Our opening vignette of the reception of *Battlefield V's* reveal trailer demonstrates how dominant some of these exclusionary, toxic traits continue to be. During the industry's formative decades, it has been the enthusiast press that gestured, guided, and sometimes even contributed to game culture's subcultural spiral—or, to put it more generously, they did little to prevent its slide into the misogynistic abyss.

Having placed gaming's subcultural roots into historical context, we switch perspectives in the next chapter, discussing how game journalists as both cultural intermediaries and passionate experts have contributed to and frustrated the mainstreaming of games.

3
Passionate Experts

What are the job requirements to be a game journalist? Historically, most have been autodidacts who rose through the ranks. Critics and reviewers commonly gained a track record by starting as unpaid volunteers for small fanzines and magazines, or more recently by writing for websites and blogs. Those with institutional aspirations may start by writing for the culture section of their local newspaper and, with some luck, eventually become a dedicated game reporter. Although rare, job postings occasionally arise for this niche position. In 2017, Vox Media—the parent company of the game website *Polygon*—was recruiting a "Games Reporter" for their New York office.[1] The job requirements were noticeably generic. They included the "ability to write quickly, clearly and accurately" and to have "familiarity with online publishing tools." Of course, the ideal candidate would have an "interest in pursuing gaming news from a variety of sources" and should "[like] video games, but also other stuff too." Curiosity and originality were deemed important, but the requirement to play games well was conspicuously absent.

Do game journalists even have to be good at playing games? It is better not to ask Dean Takahashi this question.[2] The veteran reporter is one of the few people who has occupied all three occupational roles we delineated in chapter 1—institutional journalist, game critic, and game reviewer. Takahashi has written two deeply researched books about the development of the Xbox and Xbox 360.[3] He worked for newspapers including the *San Jose Mercury News* and the *Los Angeles Times*, then moved on to write for technology blog *VentureBeat*, where he contributed more than 15,000 posts over the span of a decade. Most of his articles cover the business and technology side of the game industry, but occasionally he writes a game preview or review. In August 2017, at the German trade show Gamescom, Takahashi decided to record his first time playing *Cuphead*, a successful retro "run and gun" indie game in which the player—alone or in cooperative mode—progresses through a level by shooting everything that moves until they reach the inevitable and challenging boss fight.

In an astute piece of academic game criticism, David McGowan points to *Cuphead*'s "intense difficulty," which forces players "to continually replay and master each level in order to progress, an act which itself elicits the almost-ritualized repeat viewings of VHS tapes."[4] Standing on the showroom floor of a hectic game convention, however, meant Takahashi unfortunately did not have that luxury. Instead, he played *Cuphead* for 26 minutes, during which he, in his own words, "sucked."[5]

Figure 3.1

Dean Takahashi responds to his play of *Cuphead* with the statement that he "failed miserably." He ends the first paragraph apologizing to his readers. Source: Dean Takahashi, "Our Cuphead Runneth Over," *VentureBeat* (blog), September 8, 2017, https://venturebeat.com/2017/09/08/the-deanbeat-our-cuphead-runneth-over.

Upon his return to the United States, he shared the footage with his editors, who uploaded it to YouTube. The clip initially received a thousand views, but when a reactionary game journalist with a large following called attention to the video, the counter quickly rose to 1.6 million views. Avid players watching Takahashi's gameplay will undoubtedly yearn to reach through the screen, wrest the controller from him, and push the correct combination of buttons. Takahashi was fully aware of this fact and admitted in his comments on the *VentureBeat* blog that his performance was "shameful" (figure 3.1). Those who commented on the clip did not seem to put much stock in his tongue-in-cheek self-flagellation, however; the comments quickly devolved into insults about his mental abilities and worse.

Before we revisit the question of mainstreaming later in this chapter, we will first discuss the occupational norms and practices of game journalists. We begin by considering both their written and unwritten job requirements. Many norms, such as the expectation to be a skilled player, are rarely codified; they are not listed in the *Polygon* job ad. Skill requirements, however, are a fluid subcultural norm, the genesis of which we addressed in the previous chapter. They emerged from game magazines, are shaped by the boundary work performed by game journalists, are reinforced through online debates (and attacks), and are on full display at in-person gatherings such as Gamescom. Underlying these norms are a series of difficult questions: What counts as passion in gaming? Who are game experts? And what is expertise? To answer, we argue that passion and expertise have served as rocket fuel for digital play's tendency to alienate. Drawing on personal experiences and recent scholarly work, we argue that game journalists continuously find themselves stuck between a rock and a hard place: beholden to the industry for access to equipment and content while at the same time unsure how to determine their own occupational standards and how to effectively advocate for the medium to the wider public.[6]

Game Journalists as Cultural Intermediaries

To prevent falling into the trap of ludic essentialism— the idea that games are a special form of media—we should first consider game journalism's position within the wider domains of arts and lifestyle coverage. Game journalists share many occupational practices and norms with their peers in the film, music, food, automotive, travel, and fashion sections of news outlets. Collectively, these writers act as "cultural intermediaries": professional experts, or "tastemakers," in a position to generate, appropriate, and negotiate cultural *value* as they mediate between institutions and consumers.[7] The concept of cultural intermediaries was introduced by the French sociologist Pierre Bourdieu, who was interested in the formation, construction, and, particularly important for our understanding of mainstreaming, the *legitimation* of taste and expertise.[8]

Becoming, being, and remaining an expert is a process of constant contestation. Cultural intermediaries confer ceaselessly between producers and consumers to create value and desire. Readers need to get on board, and when writing about a fast-moving industry, so do sources and professionals. Attentiveness to this balancing act, and to the power relationships it invokes, is one of the reasons Bourdieu's work resonates so well among those who study cultural journalism. To be deemed an expert, and therefore a person worthy of attention, one must accrue social status and cultural capital: academic credentials, access to symbolic material, and cultural literacy. For Bourdieu, the ability to amass cultural capital is highly dependent on one's class position. As discussed in the previous chapter, Mia Consalvo built on these insights by demonstrating that cultural capital has its own subset in game culture: game capital.[9] This medium-specific compilation of knowledge, experiences, and literacy can be seen as a fluid currency that is shared among players, journalists, and the industry.

How game journalists accrue and subsequently deploy game capital is instructive for our concept of mainstreaming because it helps us to better understand why and how the enthusiast press has historically frustrated both game literacy and legitimacy among what Bourdieu dubs "the dominant class." In the world of journalism, the dominant class of media elites includes policy makers, opinion leaders, and mainstream news organizations, along with the institutional journalists they employ. Unlike film critics in the 1960s, game reviewers and critics never found sure footing within the confines of institutional outlets.[10] This may well be a result of their collective lack of traditional markers of cultural capital and the low status of games in the cultural hierarchy.

Although the notion of parlaying cultural value and disseminating game capital may sound abstract, the process is rather straightforward in practice. As discussed in the previous chapter, the history of game magazine publishing demonstrates that the industry, critics, and reviewers collectively catered to an increasingly narrow audience. How did this play out in practice?

Straight from the Source

In the spring of 2008, Sony needed a marketing boost. The PlayStation 3 had launched in Europe the year before, but it was clear that both Microsoft and Nintendo were giving Sony a run for its money. Sony had done incredibly well during the sixth console generation (2000–2005) with the PlayStation 2, to this day the best-selling home console ever with over 155 million units shipped. The start of the seventh console generation, however, was different. To journalists, gamers, and industry insiders' surprise, Nintendo introduced the Wii, which was a clear attempt to break with gaming's subcultural roots as it explicitly addressed a much broader audience.[11] Microsoft, for its part, was in a much better competitive position than years prior. It had learned from past mistakes and set a lower introductory price for the Xbox 360, resulting in improved sales.[12] Since Sony had invested tens of millions of dollars in its sophisticated new machine, the company felt obliged to embark on a massive PR push to rekindle consumer demand. They picked the swanky Indigo Club, part of the O2 Arena in London, to tell the European game press why the PlayStation 3 was a superior piece of technology and, taking a cue from Nintendo's recent success, why it had the potential to "broaden the market."

The president of Sony's PlayStation division, Kazuo Hirai, took the stage at the start of the press conference, stating: "Ultimately, it's the games that define the PlayStation and games that continue to excite all PlayStation and gaming fans alike."[13] I (David) sat in the back of the room, taking it all in.[14] How did I end up there? Two weeks earlier, I received a frantic call from Sony's local PR representative: "We are organizing PlayStation Day in London. Do you want to come?" Those sorts of calls became increasingly frequent as my freelance game journalism career took off and I became a regular contributor to *Dagblad De Pers*, a Dutch daily newspaper.[15] The freesheet's editorial team was relatively young and eager to shake things up. Rival outlets, particularly incumbent subscription newspapers, sparsely covered games. Conversely, the industry's subcultural aura of both innovation and deviance resonated with the general attitude among *Dagblad De Pers'* editors: "If none of the other Dutch newspapers are taking games seriously, then we definitely should!"

As a result, every week I had at least half a page at my disposal. So much real estate in a print newspaper was (and still is) a rare luxury for any institutional outlet. Sony's invitation, therefore, was most welcome. It provided me with enough material for at least one full-length (i.e., roughly 1,000 words) article, along with potential future reviews. And it was an invitation that included transportation, accommodation, and refreshments, no strings attached. Since I was a freelancer, my editors were on board with this arrangement. The newspaper was distributed for free, so we all were much more comfortable with blurring the lines between editorial content and sponsored material.

In London, Hirai's presentation was utterly unremarkable. Anybody who has seen game companies do press conferences knows how these events unfold: sales figures, announcements, subtle jabs at competitors, and a not-so-subtle nod to the free booze available after the presentation. Over a decade later, this event stands out from the rest because of what happened immediately after the presentation. As hundreds of European game journalists—truly an all-dude army—streamed out of the auditorium, I spotted some Dutch colleagues. The trio were prototypical game reviewers in their early twenties who worked for popular game websites in the Netherlands. They were recording a video report with the podium in the background, the host talking enthusiastically into the camera as if it was *he* making Sony's pitch. The host restated the company's sales figures and

ended his brief story with a Dutch translation of: "Ultimately, it's the games that define the PlayStation and
games that continue to excite all PlayStation and gaming fans alike."

After the reviewer trio wrapped up, I walked over and
asked them how they felt about the event. Feeling cyni-
cal after so much empty PR, I hoped they could offer me
some fresh insights. They gushed over the fancy cock-
tails and snacks, beautiful hostesses, and the opportunity to play a slew of unreleased titles! It was rumored
that Sony executives and developers might join the press
for (more) drinks later that evening. A huge chunk of
game capital was about to fall into their laps. This is why
they covered games (without pay) in the first place. Free
games, free trips, free booze, and hanging out with bud-
dies from across the continent. What was not to like?

Later that night, together with a dozen members of
the gaming press, we stumbled to our hotel. Sony's local
PR representative did his best to keep the intoxicated
Dutch mob under control. I was heading to my room,
but the poor marketing manager was not done for the
night. The afterparty continued in the hotel lobby,
which quickly turned into a makeshift bar. "We need
more beer!" one older game reviewer demanded. The PR
guy obliged—anything to keep his merry band of misfits
happy. After all, he would need their collective goodwill
later that year for the release of the blockbuster game
Killzone 2, which was developed in Amsterdam.

Free as in Free Beer

What to make of the London event? For starters, its setup was far from unique, nor was the willingness of game journalists to take part. This occupational disposition was—and still is, to some extent—similar to the practices of lifestyle journalists who cover bands, visit far-flung cities, or write about fancy meals in chic restaurants.[16] As we noted in chapter 1, however, the code of conduct among game reviewers is quite different from those of institutional reporters. The former provides soft news meant to entertain and advise (e.g., buy a game), whereas "professional" hard news journalists are tasked with being objective and rational and abiding by a clear set of ethics.[17] In practice, the hard/soft news dichotomy breaks down rather quickly. Severin Poirot observes that game journalists themselves contribute to this blurriness:

> The term journalist seems to be variable based on who is using and who is applying the term. Some individuals identify as a journalist . . . Others did not consider what they did as journalism or themselves as journalists. They suggested that they were "critics" and that what they did was opinion.[18]

What this clear example shows is that the line separating political coverage—the holy grail of institutional journalism—from lifestyle journalism and cultural criticism, along with what each of these groups consider to be ethical, is constantly shifting. Even among the different genres of lifestyle journalism (e.g., sports, travel, food, and health) there are stark differences; every type "follows its specific professional routines and economic conditions."[19] For example, my own PlayStation Day story shows that even those who write for a daily newspaper—arguably the last refuge of institutional journalism—can easily cross ethical or professional boundaries deemed taboo at other publications. One such ethically fraught decision would be for a reporter to accept anything of monetary value, such as an all-expenses-paid two-day trip to downtown London.

The point here is not that game journalists are morally bankrupt, unethical individuals who, in exchange for free booze and swag, provide favorable coverage. In practice, the relationship between the industry and game journalists is much more organic. Because of their institutional proximity to the industry, game journalists aspire to be transparent about "informing their audience of what they may have received for their participation" in corporate events.[20] Many are well aware of their unique position as cultural intermediaries and aim to be truthful in their reporting. That said, there is an implied quid pro quo—if not a massive power imbalance—between the industry and the press.

The simple truth about game journalism in the subcultural era is that the relationship between the industry and journalists is symbiotic. As cultural intermediaries, what game journalists mediate

> continues to be filtered by the market; their ability to sell advertising space and to produce subscribers and site visits—attracting readers with full and detailed, if not "world exclusive" coverage accompanied by large, glossy game play stills and interviews with game developers—remains dependent on the positive benefits of working closely, if not entirely ethically, with producers.[21]

For decades, this mutually beneficial, transactional relationship resulted in an agreed-upon equilibrium. Game journalists do not participate in some hidden, well-devised, nefarious scheme aimed at self-enrichment. Reviewers are not forced to take lavish trips around the world. If one does consider accepting nonmonetary rewards as an ethical breach—and there is absolutely something to be said for such a strict professional stance—such breaches have happened for decades, out in the open and for all to see.[22]

There may be those who seem to think that such ethical lapses are anomalies, but none of what we have described so far will be new or shocking to those who have read game magazines or frequented online outlets over the last three decades. In the case of the PlayStation Day, many of the Dutch writers present loudly and proudly recounted the trip in our respective publications, ranging from enthusiast magazines and websites to mainstream newspapers. So did our Spanish, Danish, and British peers. After all, industry events provide the perfect background for an entertaining blog post or video report that mixes travel journalism (we are in

London!), with useful data (PlayStation sales figures), and some mild tongue-in-cheek criticism. All this is to say, game publishers wield a weapon much more powerful than outright bribery: access to exclusive resources such as press events, unreleased games, and opportunities to meet directly with industry professionals.

We point to these fraught institutional arrangements because they are so clearly at odds with journalistic norms, from objective reporting to critical distance. What irks us are not so much these arrangements but rather the relentless vitriol from accusers (i.e., fans and core gamers) against those whose behavior is said to breach occupational norms. We are the first to welcome good-faith debates about ethics and objectivity. It is part of what motivated us to write this book. Yet, the disproportionate number of attacks on female, trans, and nonbinary game developers, journalists, pundits, and academics for their supposed ethics breaches do not square with the decades-long history of the enthusiast press we have just described. Put differently, those who are concerned about "ethics in games journalism" are awfully selective in their anger about actual ethical violations.

Apart from underscoring how the public occupational practices of game journalists are admittedly unshackled from traditional journalistic norms, we want to emphasize industry and audience complicity in setting and reifying these cultural norms and occupational expectations. Readers of the enthusiast press expect critics and reviewers to be close with industry insiders. Throughout my decade as a game journalist, readers never questioned who paid for those lavish trips, who got access to which company, and why. On the contrary! In game websites' comments sections, fans openly applaud reviewers for their "hard work," or their willingness to fly to faraway lands, play new games quickly, and report back without breaking the unwritten rule of smothering a title's momentum before release. Add to this that members of the enthusiast press are also almost always fellow consumers. Like their audience, they are gamers who just happen to be among the lucky few allowed "in."

This observation brings us to the occupational challenges faced by game journalists, which we will cover in the next two chapters. The political economy of game journalism makes the livelihood of writers inherently precarious. Sure, traveling around the world for free is fun, but out of the dozen Dutchies in London, only two or three were paid a decent salary for their efforts. The rest were freelancers, interns, or voluntary contributors. Our thin veneer of rambunctiousness hid a deep, collective sense of anxiety—not only about our (unpaid) work but also about our dependency on the industry for continued access to events, review material, and many other scraps of exclusive information constituting valuable game capital.[23] Adding insult to injury, many of the press outlets represented at the talk counted companies such as Sony as key advertisers. For some, the threat of major game companies declining to purchase advertising, to prevent participation in press junkets, or to restrict access to early copies—an industry practice known as "blackballing"—served as an effective deterrent against overly critical coverage. Whenever I met fellow Dutch game journalists, we openly talked about one or two notorious PR reps who had no qualms about "pulling somebody through the phone" if they did not like their work. In many respects, game journalism remains mired in the same kinds of controversies that marked late nineteenth-century journalism, when advertisers dictated "puff" pieces and advertising "functioned essentially as a bribe."[24]

In sum, the ability of game journalists to connect with an audience that appreciates their expertise has been directly tied to their ability to leverage game capital. Many core gamers do not seem to crave cultural legitimacy (i.e., mainstream acceptance) but rather desire validation and acknowledgment, however implicit, of their dedication and passion. In return, readers ask— and at times violently demand—that their favorite reviewers and critics match or exceed their level of dedication and skill.

Passion, Expertise, and Legitimacy

By cultivating a very specific understanding of passion and dedication, both fans and game critics helped erect one of the three major barriers to mainstreaming.

The British scholar Jamie Woodcock explains that the "mobilization of passion" permeates game culture and is "something that begins in the consumption, rather than production of videogames."[25] To an extent, the passion requirement concerns all cultural intermediaries. They all "are taste makers and legitimation authorities because of their personal investment in the work."[26] Yet, arguably more so than other forms of cultural criticism, the practice of game criticism is explicitly tied to skill—or, more precisely, the expectation of hyperliteracy and possession of the "right" skills. Although movie and music critics may have expertise because of their canonical knowledge, we would typically not say that they are skillful or "good" at watching movies or listening to (or even playing) music. To be seen as a ludic expert, by contrast, one must demonstrate the ability to play "well." As the chapter's opening example illustrates, what playing well means is not only highly subjective but also deeply political. A game journalist publicly demonstrating an inability to play well—by not progressing in a level, for instance—instantly invalidates their legitimacy as an expert in the eyes of many core gamers.

For reviewers, a host of practical issues exacerbates the requirement to be deemed skillful. They must be able to finish a game quickly and effectively, be it a demo or the final release. Whatever medium one writes for, there still are deadlines to meet and competitors to think about. Add to this the lack of professional credentials; there are few university degrees, certificates, or textbooks for critics. This lack of standards makes game journalism more appealing as a career option for younger players. They may consider their gaming ability to equal or even surpass that of the average reviewer. If there are no diplomas or other external validation mechanisms, skill and subcultural knowledge become vital markers of expertise.

Specific skill requirements help explain why passion frustrates game literacy. Because a game journalist's legitimacy is partly derived from attaining a high level of game literacy, there are few incentives for reviewers to critique a game's inaccessibility to outsiders. Quite the opposite, in fact—a large contingent of reviewers and critics are quick to scorn games that do not require skill or significant investment of time and effort. A "real game" is held to be "immersive, rich, and deep," meaning that they are long (allowing for many hours of play), played on certain platforms (PC or consoles), and have a "perceived difficulty" that is "appropriate and valued."[27] Even in mainstream game criticism, we rarely see open acknowledgments of how hard it is to navigate virtual worlds. For example, in his op-ed for the *New York Times'* Sunday review, Peter Suderman attempts to convince readers that the Western-themed blockbuster game *Red Dead Redemption 2* is "true art."[28] He does so by appealing to all the aforementioned "real game" tropes, such as technical achievement and an unprecedented development budget. In addition, he puts the game on the same cultural pedestal as other forms of high culture by describing it as "richly cinematic and even literary."[29] What Suderman does not do, however, is acknowledge the game's inherent inaccessibility. For recurrent players, the game may be a breeze, but newcomers who want to navigate its vast virtual world face a steep learning curve. In other words, even if one is swayed by Suderman's sweeping praise, one must be digitally literate to play the game effectively. What he provides in cultural legitimacy by publishing in the *New York Times* comes at the expense of game literacy.

Boundary Policing in a World of Extremes

Although being passionate has a positive connotation, studies of digital culture demonstrate that passion can also be harnessed or misdirected toward nefarious ends, pushing out supposed nonbelievers and measuring legitimacy based on constantly shifting metrics.[30] In a blogpost reflecting on the personal attacks following *Cuphead*-gate, Takahashi touts his many decades as an unwavering fan. He was credible, he assumed, because he was one of them, a dedicated expert deeply and personally invested: "In all of my 45 years or so as a gamer—yep, since the original Pong came out—nobody ever denied that I was a proper and legitimate game fan. Until now."[31] He then noted that his editors never cared about him being good at playing: "They required basic knowledge and competence, but not skill on an esports level." The *Cuphead* episode reinforces what decades of game journalism history demonstrate about how gamers and a subset of reviewers actively police both the boundaries of their subcultural domain and those who are allowed to critique it.

When considering a cultural form's accessibility, passion among its mediators is a double-edged sword directly tied to race and gender. All forms of cultural criticism come from a place of intrinsic fascination. As a reviewer, one cannot marshal passion and loyalty if one despises the very act of playing. Too much passion, however, can be more destructive; there is a fine line between enthusiasm and aggression, and a clear line between bias and bigotry. For instance, what should be a foregone conclusion is still very much an open question in practice: can women be game reviewers? As argued by Adrienne Shaw, not only is it hard for women to simply be present in male-dominated spaces, such as game studios and trade shows, they are also "flat out rejected to critique games as cultural texts."[32]

What does this exclusionary stance look like in practice? In his tell-all book *Sex, Drugs, and Cartoon Violence: My Decade as a Video Game Journalist*, Russ Pitts states that the game industry's gender ratio is 10:1 in "favor of men," which is one reason why "the strip club is a perennial favorite locale in the game industry. The girls are already there."[33] There are women who work as game developers, but they are far outnumbered by men.[34]

Female executives working at dominant game publishers are virtually nonexistent. This gender disparity mirrors broader trends in the media industries, as the media sociologist Brooke Erin Duffy notes: "While men dominate more prestigious creative roles as well as technical and craft fields, women are concentrated in marketing, communications, and service roles."[35] We see similar gender dynamics among members of the enthusiast press. Most of the women visible to game journalists, according to Nina Huntemann, do not work in "design, development, or executive positions" but rather have promotional roles.[36] The fact that until very recently some members of the latter group worked as "booth babes," who were a large presence at major industry events, should be indicative enough of the "hotbed of rampant sexism and misogyny" that Pitts describes.[37]

The presence of promotional models at trade events is exactly the kind of marker that depresses cultural validity. Not only does it signal that such key events are male-dominated spaces but it is also part of a deeply subcultural promotional strategy. Would the literary critic of a mainstream newspaper expect to encounter a "book babe" at an industry event? Pitts recounts how industry leader Sony promoted its 2007 blockbuster action game *God of War* "by throwing a party at which topless models fed grapes to visiting journalists and a live goat was slaughtered and decapitated, for fun."[38] There are few things worse for granting mainstream legitimacy than mixing gratuitous sexism with animal abuse.

For whom, then, do typical game critics and reviewers write? Who is the ideal consumer of a game review or essay? The simplest answer should arguably be those who play, which would ultimately represent most sociocultural categories—who doesn't play? Yet, in the mid-2000s, the readership of game magazines was said to have "an overwhelmingly male readership, usually in the 90 to 95 percent range."[39] In addition, most game reviewers and critics are recruited from that very pool of core game consumers. These exclusionary publishing practices may profit both magazine and game publishers, but they exact a heavy toll on individual writers.

A Culture of Anxiety

A growing body of scholarship points to a perplexing professional conundrum. Game journalists lack confidence in their occupational role (are they even journalists?) and in the longevity of their jobs because they face an enduring deficit of legitimacy as long as they are shackled to subcultural outlets. In some ways, such concerns are not unusual for those at the "margins of the journalistic field," such as music writers, who also have deep industry ties.[40] In game journalism, however, the absolute dependence on publishers and fellow gamers has resulted in the institutional press considering it "a lower, marginal form" with core tenets that lie at the fringes of what is deemed proper journalism.[41]

Howard Fisher and Sufyan Mohammed-Baksh characterize this constant strain and resultant occupational
ambivalence as an "ideology of anxiety."[42] Game journalists have collectively internalized concerns over their
professional standing. This not only takes a mental toll
but also influences their writing, which is characterized as "preemptively obedient" and is used "as a way of
denying responsibility for some of the things they write
and for their role in maintaining the status quo."[43] Seen
in this light, anxiety, a mass inferiority complex, and
an abdication of responsibility on the part of writers,
industry, and gamers all contributed to the debacle that
came to be known as Gamergate.

Because of our distaste for the events themselves, not
to mention the surfeit of media coverage and research,
we prefer not to linger over the events as they unfolded
in 2014 and 2015. Essentially, under the aegis of combating issues of "ethics in games journalism," an ad
hoc group of mostly anonymous self-identified gamers
intimidated those whom they judged to be endanger-
ing "real" games, particularly nonmale developers and
scholars. From the insularity of media platforms such
as Reddit, Twitter, and 4chan, loosely formed online
groups initiated actions that have become sadly com-
monplace in political life, beginning with online attacks
such as "doxxing" and moving rapidly to more serious
forms of harassment such as "SWATing" and bomb
threats.[44] Despite Gamergate's outsized media coverage,
many of the issues surrounding the 2014 summer of

hate were unexceptional in game culture. Other "-gates" had come before, and more followed. As media studies scholar Amanda C. Cote points out, the events were "a symptom of deeper structures of sexism and backlash in gaming."[45] Add to that the pervasive racist undercurrent that permeates online game communities, which was present long before 2014.[46]

It is the journalistic response to Gamergate and its manifestation of the endemic problems of game journalism that we want to highlight.[47] Gamergate's impact was expansive: many quit the industry rather than face further assaults. Others deeply reflected on the toxicity of game culture more broadly. Scholars Shira Chess and Adrienne Shaw advocated that academics rethink how they communicate these issues to the public.[48] Torill Mortensen focused on the embedded problems of "geek masculinity" to which most aggressors adhered.[49] If this abasement seems eerily familiar to the uninitiated, it is because as much as Gamergate might have been inevitable, it is also widely considered to be a testing ground for many of the misogynistic tactics of the extreme right in North America and of other bad-faith actors across the globe. That is, Gamergate was emblematic not only of structural social inequities but also of the failure of social media platforms, journalists, politicians, and others to effectively counter toxic cultural sects.

Immediately following the summer of 2014, game journalists were conflicted about how to cover Gamergate. They tried to tread a cautious line between explaining the movement to their core audience while also adopting what the journalism professors Gregory Perrault and Tim Vos regard as "the role of traditional journalist[s], linking themselves with established journalistic entities and practices."[50] Journalists struggled to hold those in power accountable while also maintaining their subcultural positions as passionate experts. Gamergate proponents collectively sensed this contradiction, forcing game journalists and publishers to take an explicit stand. Ironically, when they did so, the brunt of the subsequent harassment was faced by individual developers and reporters, not the industry.

In the end, the trolls driving Gamergate were quite successful in their efforts to exploit the professional weaknesses of game journalists in a broader attempt to demean underrepresented communities in the field, including women, people of color, and other marginalized groups. Because of the subcultural status of games and the industry's strict supervision of their occupational boundaries, journalists could neither fully fulfill their role as a bulwark nor check this phenomenon.[51] Although Gamergate as an active community became less effective in the ensuing years, it impelled game publications to reexamine their function in a rapidly changing media landscape. As editors reviewed their newsroom tactics and policies, new modes of game journalism emerged, which we will address in greater detail in the next chapter.

4
The Many Streams of Game Journalism

"The most interesting things about games, to general readers, are often not the things we fixate on in video-game world, for better and for worse," concluded Keza MacDonald in a public confession on Twitter announcing her move from game website *Kotaku* to UK-based newspaper the *Guardian*.[1] After a decade of professional experience, MacDonald reflected animatedly about the transition to a traditional newspaper where there was less "uniformly positive" industry coverage. Her work now catered to less informed audiences who had no idea what modern games were like and did not care about technical features, like graphic fidelity or smooth controls. Casting herself as a diplomat, MacDonald's tweets indicate that, for the "*average*" reader, games remain mysterious, unappealing, and maybe even harmful.

Many of our interviewees concurred with Mac-Donald's outlook. As discussed in the introduction, we had twenty conversations with writers and editors from both enthusiast and institutional outlets to better understand the landscape of contemporary game journalism. We asked them a variety of questions, ranging from their perceived roles as game journalists to the stylistic choices they made in writing stories to their thoughts about the mainstreaming of games. Respondents believed that games were "growing up" and that in the next decade they might even warrant "serious" coverage and critique. "Games are really young. They are still maturing. I think the most prominent games that people see and what they see about them are [not displayed] in the best light," said former *Kill Screen* editor and writer Clayton Purdom. With this potential looming, those whom we interviewed felt that in the interim they must take on the conciliatory role that MacDonald suggested.

Then again, should we consider a fifty-year-old medium to still be in its infancy? And why do we require emissaries from virtual worlds in the first place? Some of the answers to these questions can be traced to the media ecosystem that MacDonald and her peers inhabit. The days of finding out about the latest releases from *GamePro* or *Nintendo Power* are long gone, as are those magazines. Instead, algorithmically curated evaluations from YouTube, TikTok, or Twitch creators may be the first piece of gameplay audiences encounter before anything appears in enthusiast publications, let alone institutional news outlets. As a result, instead of diplomats, this fractured environment produces occupational nomads. To establish themselves, some game journalists still lean heavily into the subcultural norms we discussed in earlier chapters. Others are slowly adapting their work around the professional boundaries and ideologies we discussed in chapter 1.

To account for the different roles game journalists occupy, in this chapter we introduce four occupational archetypes: 1) entertainers, 2) enthusiast critics, 3) game beat reporters, and 4) institutional journalists. We situate each within the contemporary media landscape and reflect on how they exploit the industry-supported sub-cultural capital discussed in earlier chapters. Crucially, we emphasize that each type simultaneously expands *and* constricts the legitimacy, literacy, and ubiquity of games in the public imagination in different ways. Because of that, we further the argument that, combined, these four types challenge the effectiveness of game journalists as mainstream cultural intermediaries altogether.

To better understand how these four types fit into a shattered contemporary information ecosystem, we start by describing how the growth of digital platforms has challenged journalistic standards and created a precarious situation for practitioners. Writers must compete in a wide variety of arenas where they bank on knowledge of games for reviewing and reporting. The ongoing process of "platformization"—during which news production becomes "platform-dependent"—unfolds alongside the industry-wide practice of freelancing.[2] This way of working, where writers rely on their own ability to find and pitch story ideas to different platforms, and are often paid by the word in the process, provides the economic foundation for most outlets to persist, particularly as they downsize their staff. Freelancing also reverberated in our interviews as being instrumental to the way reporters approach and produce content.

Playing with Platforms

The metamorphosis of game journalism, as well as events like Gamergate, did not occur in a vacuum. They are both a source and symptom of an ongoing "crisis" that mainstream publications find themselves in. Due in part to the 2008 financial recession and to revenue losses as print newspapers moved online, the number of US newsrooms has steadily declined, shedding over half of their employees between 2008 and 2019 while other news-producing industries, such as television and radio, saw a modest rise.[3]

Because a majority of Americans get their news digitally, countless publications are subject to the economic, infrastructural, and governmental whims of digital platforms, Facebook and Google in particular, typically without necessarily reaping proportional rewards.[4] Scholars suggest that such instances of platform dependency have precipitated a reassessment of the audience–publisher relationship, journalistic independence, and the very value of news coverage itself.[5] Reporting is less valuable when breaking news can be gleaned from social media, and journalists' freelancing careers may be measured through Twitter posts as much as bylines.

What does all of this mean for mainstreaming? Journalists and cultural critics have often played a vital role in deciding what is mainstream. Yet, because even the most entrenched institutions are dependent on platforms, it is increasingly difficult to distinguish "mainstream" journalism from more niche outlets, or even from the "vernacular amateurs" who replicate the work of professional reporters in their reviews.[6] Instead, the media landscape is much more atomized; there are only a handful of national outlets in the United States that garner massive audiences, and the remaining news content emanates from a hodgepodge of sources. Game journalism resides in this increasingly blurred platform-dependent environment that neither needs nor is inherently inclined to support traditional coverage. At the same time, like many of their institutional counterparts, game publications and writers increasingly rely on platforms and niche audiences to remain viable. These circumstances create opportunities for enthusiast game outlets to advance more serious reportage.

The Game Publishing Landscape

The economic and occupational challenges rising from a changing media landscape altered the occupation and output of contemporary game journalists. Platforms broke simple binaries between the enthusiast press and institutional organizations and the way each report about games. National newspapers no longer write solely about video game addiction and violence; enthusiast sites now include multiyear investigative pieces; and social media platforms have created a bottomless reservoir of both reviewers and critics. The democratization of news production and distribution upends the traditional role of game journalists as cultural intermediaries; they are no longer the only, let alone the primary, arbiters of taste. Indeed, written content in general has been superseded by other formats, in particular the explosion of videos on YouTube, TikTok, Snapchat, and Twitch.[7] Scholars Mark Johnson and Jamie Woodcock categorized live streaming as "a new form of game reviewing" that disrupts the critical role of the reviewer in favor of being able to speak directly to audiences and showcase more gameplay.[8] When it comes to cultural criticism, video streaming and game reviews are perceived to be a perfect match.

That said, despite being most affected by new modes of coverage, enthusiast online outlets like *GameSpot* and *IGN* still rank among the top-visited websites in the world.[9] They retain many of the traditional enthusiast press's trappings we described earlier, including the preview and review formats. The continued relevance of enthusiast sites, Johnson and Woodcock argue, does not mean that consumers are fixated on one type of content over the other. Instead, each serves a different purpose:

audiences rely on reviewers' expertise whereas they self-identify with streamers. Put differently, the former is about taste formation and legitimation; the latter serves as entertainment.

Along with streaming platforms, a bumper crop of novel online news organizations has risen to challenge the dominance of incumbent game magazines. One could consider them niche sites. *Inverse*, for instance, covers "geek" culture and reports on a wide variety of entertainment including comics, computer tech, and games (along with such topics as science and innovation). Others are decidedly game focused, such as *Kotaku*, *Polygon*, and the *Verge*, all of which also happen to be verticals of larger news media groups: *Kotaku* was part of Gawker Media during its heyday (and now exists under the G/O Media umbrella), and the others are owned by Vox Media. Propagated by websites such as *Critical Distance*, these newcomers claim to assess games with more "incisive, thought-provoking, and remarkable" coverage compared to incumbent enthusiast outlets.[10] Niche reporting also counterbalances the more indiscriminate coverage spawned by mainstream institutions. Some legacy publications, such as the *Wall Street Journal*, have long covered the business of games, and others, such as the *Guardian*, have a dedicated game section. The *Washington Post* notably introduced an entire vertical, Launcher, devoted to games and esports in 2019, and there is no shortage of permutations in between. Other mainstream outlets expect their science or technology columnists to include this topic in their bailiwicks.

In summary, tectonic shifts in the media industries and the rise of platforms disrupted the traditional publishing ecosystem while blurring and displacing the roles held by both enthusiast and institutional news sites. Game information, ranging from serious reporting to entertaining playthroughs, can be garnered from a diffuse set of authorities. Although this profusion of outlets may allow audiences easier access to a wider variety of content, it complicates the role and self-perception of journalists, especially freelancers.[11] The latter category of occupational wanderers has become among some of the most impassioned voices of coverage and criticism. Therefore, before discussing the four archetypes of game journalists below, we first survey the role of freelancers—an occupational meta-category in which each of the four archetypes may fall.

Freelancing and Professional Insecurity

Like many innovations at the heart of the gig economy, social media platforms left writers unmoored, jockeying between publishers for jobs. To be sure, Facebook, Google, and Apple did not start the casualization of work—freelancers have long been part and parcel of news production—but platformization certainly increased the ranks of those without full-time positions.[12] To survive, freelancing game journalists don many hats, fighting for the medium's relevance at one organization while articulating game minutiae for another. They must modulate their authorial voices for distinctly different readers based on the frame and format in which they are writing. We discuss the economic precarity of freelancers in greater depth in chapter 5, but here we stress that they remain the economic backbone of game coverage. The hiring of full-time game writers would do much to legitimize the mainstream acceptance of the genre. Instead, prominent publications have dabbled with but ultimately retreated from funding permanent positions.[13]

In addition to having widely different orientations, abilities, and backgrounds, all of which directly color their writing, a lack of job security means freelancers are also destined to be inconsistently trained in professional norms and ethics. We have written elsewhere about the ongoing ambivalence among game writers about their vocation, which raises the persistent question of what type of writer they should be: a critic, a journalist, or a game reviewer?[14] Their indecision can be attributed to the occupational precarity that comes from instability; rather than finding cohesive benchmarks by which to practice their craft, writers remain in stylistic limbo, adjusting to contradictory demands and bouncing between regional, niche, and mainstream publications, all the while trying to build a portfolio that they can leverage for future employment. Because they hop from gig to gig, the length and depth of work varies; some freelancers toil for months on a longstanding exposé while others scratch out a living from a steady stream of reviews and other forms of commentary, such as calling esports tournaments. Thus, freelancers fuel the ubiquity of game coverage even as their precarity strains the legitimacy of the medium and literacy among its audiences.

If such frustrations preoccupied authors, the editors we talked to affirmed freelancers' value. Former *Kotaku* writer Harper Jay MacIntyre observed, "What you see on smaller sites where budgets are actually very limited is an outsourcing to freelancers because they have particular areas of interest and very particular pitches that can be used for future articles." Freelancers' passion is a boon to publications because they can be assigned work that will "occupy the majority of their attention," MacIntyre added. Journalist and professor Evan Narcisse disclosed the specialized knowledge necessary for such a writer. He asked us to name five people who might know the "general design direction" of a game franchise, similar to the directors of major motion pictures, and added, "Unless you follow video game journalism and critique and conversations on a day-to-day basis, most people can't do that." Editors stated, however, that since they tend to hire freelancers on a "rotational basis," long-standing relationships are tenuous at best. This further damages how institutional reporters perceive game journalists, the latter of whom do not necessarily develop connections, skills, and occupational ideologies through daily newsroom work. Thus, they cannot do the boundary work described in chapter 1. Instead, under the guise of alleged autonomy, freelancers spend hours hustling, networking, pitching, and relying on various platforms for exposure.[15] Simply put, they cannot afford to have defined boundaries if their livelihood is contingent on being hired on a job-by-job basis.

Four Types of Contemporary Game Journalists

Contemporary game journalists' work falls along a broad spectrum of writing styles, genres, institutional affiliations, and occupational ideologies. Based primarily on the interviews conducted, we distinguish four types of game journalists: *entertainers*, who leverage subcultural game capital that historically has been accrued and disseminated via the enthusiast press; *enthusiast critics*, who have grown into their role as cultural intermediaries; *game beat reporters*, who employ institutional practices to cover game content; and *institutional journalists*, who work within the confines of legacy news organizations. These categories are ideal types that allow us to have a more granular conversation about the opportunities and challenges to the mainstreaming of games and their coverage. Since they are derived from journalists' observations, they may not reflect how audiences perceive writers.[16] Nonetheless, our categorization provides a roadmap for how game journalists tend to traverse a tangled media ecosystem.

Entertainers. For audiences of a certain age, the notorious Felix "PewDiePie" Kjellberg needs no introduction. In 2013, with 15 million subscribers, Kjellberg became the most followed YouTuber in the world. He rose to fame through his quirky "Let's Play" videos, in which he films his playthroughs of various video games, along with (off-)color commentary and jokes, to increasing levels of infamy.[17] Part preview, part review, Let's Plays are heavily imbued with the sort of subcultural game capital we discussed in chapter 2.[18] Players like Kjellberg must navigate skillfully through any popular genre. He must make it look easy, all while ranting, giggling, yelling, chiding others, swearing, and making fun of himself.[19] The genre has propelled the celebrity of countless YouTube personalities: in 2019, four of the top ten highest-earning YouTubers each made over US$10 million a year for playing and commenting on games.[20]

Entertainers like Kjellberg are personality-driven content creators who are watched primarily for fun, like any other influencer or lifestyle producer on YouTube, Twitch, or TikTok. And it is specifically YouTube that has prompted changes in game journalism over the last decade, according to our interviewees. Game reporter Jason Schreier (most recently of *Bloomberg*) insisted that it was the platform's popularity that contributed to "the rise of [game] publishers trying to control their own messages and putting out their own video and blogs. As a result of that, you've seen a lot of game sites that didn't keep up and at times struggle." Game writer and *New Yorker* contributor Simon Parkin stated it was "incredibly useful for video game publishers because now they can use YouTubers to speak directly to audiences and mediate access to trailers and information . . ." Clearly, amateur content produced by YouTube entertainers—and often endorsed by the industry—has shaken enthusiast publications, prompting Parkin to ask, "When so much of the role that traditionally the game press, both mainstream and specialist, had is now being performed by YouTubers, what do people see as the role of video game coverage?"

One thing is certain: advertising-driven platforms like YouTube incentivize entertainers to directly connect with audiences. Akin to "relational labor" in the music industry—the continuous work of musicians to connect with their audiences—"entrepreneurial journalism" is demonstrative of how entertainers' work and living become linked to incessant self-promotion.[21] It is up to individuals to amass an audience and gain access to game content without the institutional backing of news organizations. First and foremost, this necessitates yoking themselves to an industry that still parsimoniously doles out favors. For entertainers, much the same as their enthusiast press predecessors, receiving promotional material or early access to a game is not only a major perk but a professional necessity; online influencers walk a tightrope between relatability and "authentically" appraising games all while coordinating with the industries that make them.[22]

To enhance their authenticity, entertainers lean into rather than away from audiences, who socially and economically invest in them by subscribing to their channels, clicking on embedded advertisements, and so on. Entertainer commentary is consequently peppered with lingo, jokes, and memes from game culture. Games are praised or panned based on conventional rubrics of playability, and entertainers showcase their fluency with the medium by literally playing through games in response to their audiences. The growth of live streaming, helped in part by the game-focused platform Twitch, allows all of this to occur in real time alongside a barrage of criticism from vocal gamers. We saw the impact of such scrutiny on journalists such as Dean Takahashi in chapter 3, where audiences had an expectation of adequate, if not exceptional, gameplay.

When evaluating their impact on the mainstreaming of game coverage, entertainers clearly contribute to its ubiquity. Live streaming and Let's Play videos have become a go-to form of entertainment: over 63 percent of 18- to 34-year-olds watch regularly.[23] With gaming being the focus of a significant amount of streaming content, these numbers suggest that entertainers are certainly contributing to games' mainstream acceptance. It has yet to be seen, however, whether they are able to boost game literacy. Likewise, we have seen little indication that entertainers enhance the medium's legitimacy. Much of their content is off the radar, incomprehensible, and perhaps even repugnant to older generations. Generally, entertainers show little appetite to seek out such audiences, partly because they are reliant on and crave legitimacy from their followers and subscribers—not parents, pundits, or politicians. Thus, entertainers still depend heavily on subcultural practices, language, and tropes that tend to be off-putting or impenetrable to outsiders. In other words, entertainers remain gamers par excellence.

Enthusiast critics. Although Simon Parkin spent most of his career as a freelancer, he is an inveterate game critic and reporter who has authored pieces for such institutions as the *New Yorker*, the *Guardian*, and *Eurogamer*. In his work, Parkin aims to bring traditional storytelling elements to broader audiences. For example, his reason to pen a longform essay (figure 4.1) about the juggernaut series *FIFA* for the *Guardian's* "Long Reads" section was: "You can catch everyone who's interested in video game football and everyone who's interested in football." Expansively surveying the game's history, Parkin's story contains everything from a sweeping overview of the game's impact on professional soccer to a deeply personal narrative of the franchise developer Jan Tian's travails to get home to see his dying father. The result was a feature that "did really, really well" on a mainstream news site, timed as it was with the annual

theguardian

The long read
Fifa: the video game that changed football

Fifa belongs to a select group of titles familiar to people who have no interest in gaming - or even real football. What's the secret of its success?

by Simon Parkin

Figure 4.1
Enthusiast critic Simon Parkin's feature story on the *FIFA* soccer game series for the *Guardian* is for those with "no interest in gaming." Source: Simon Parkin, "Fifa: The Video Game That Changed Football," *Guardian*, December 21, 2016, http://www.theguardian.com /technology/2016/dec/21/fifa-video-game-changed-football.

release of the new *FIFA* installment around Christmas 2016. What is striking about the article is how carefully and transparently Parkin moves between stories of people (developers, publishers, and players), industry, and gameplay. Being acutely aware of the *Guardian*'s potential audience, his language is evocative even when describing the technical side of the game: "Most years, [*FIFA*] swings between a more simulation-based approach—with keenly realistic physics that generally allow for fewer goals—and a more impressionistic, playful take, in which it is easier to score screamers from 30 yards, and matches can finish with double-digit scores."[24] This is not a preview for a limited gamer public but rather one directed at the masses.

The role of enthusiast critics is decidedly different from entertainers, with the former's work significantly bolstering both the legitimacy *and* literacy of video games within public discourse. Some critics now foster increasingly inclusive language that purposely targets broader audiences. Further, they create and adhere to a set of common norms at a personal and editorial level. Unfortunately, however, these types of enthusiast critics are an elite community composed of writers possessing the occupational standing to devote their time to the long-form writing that comprises informed cultural criticism. Seen in this light, writers like Parkin are representative of the enthusiast critic's maturation.

The growth of freelancing and independent news platforms has allowed for more meaningful takes on games because new outlets needed to distinguish their coverage from incumbent institutions. No longer forced to abide by the rubrics of game reviews, enthusiast critics are freer to pursue more diverse subject matter. At the same time, however, their target audience still tends to be players, with the most detailed essays appearing in niche rather than mainstream outlets. Only a few writers straddle both worlds. Editors and writers noted the evolution and increased independence of coverage.

"Not every outlet should cover gaming," said one writer via email, adding hopefully, "I think it's starting to be taken more seriously and a lot of progress has been made on that front in recent years." They recognized that this shift meant striking a balance for their audiences and a potential for greater readership, as noted by Harper Jay MacIntyre: "You do get that tension between people who just want to sit down after a day's work, crack open a beer, and play *Call of Duty* or whatever. Then you have people who want to see games as a cultural institution or artistic medium."

In this context, editors encourage enthusiast critics to "approach things with a sense of empathy for how games are made, how they're played, and who plays them," as *Polygon* cofounder Chris Plante put it, adding, "we try to create a site that . . . feels accessible, whether that is to the most hardcore game developer, or my mother trying to find out what she should get me for Christmas, or my grandmother who just likes to play video games." Editors may make basic assumptions of readers' game literacy, such as knowing what a first-person shooter is, but they have indicated a wish to broaden rather than shrink their readership. The wider audience was also reflected in Schreier's perspective: "I see my role as trying to entertain people, trying to inform people, trying to get people stories they won't be able to read otherwise." This desire for inclusivity was not solely about the bottom line but was also a political decision. A few interviewees confessed to amending their missions post-Gamergate. Plante discussed how he thought it was important to structurally reassess "from the ground up" game journalism's voice and orientation. It also manifested in setting more standards and writing codes of conduct for critics, something we will touch upon in the next chapter. "When it comes to other ethical decisions," MacIntyre attested while working at their former employer *Kotaku*, "we disclose and we are transparent about anything that might even perceptually affect how people see our coverage."

These comments reveal the tension between functioning as a traditional cultural intermediary and applying a game critic's subcultural norms. While couching their work in the ability to inform audiences, critics acknowledge the entertainment value of their writing to gamers. Thus, enthusiast critics are very much at the vanguard of buttressing a common literacy as well as the legitimacy of games. They crisscross gaming subcultures and the mainstream, finding individual stories, such as Parkin's, to bring these disparate cultures together. It is precisely this fluidity, however, that causes enthusiast critics to be a hindrance to ubiquitous game coverage; as freelancers, they ultimately must attune their work for whatever platform they are writing, which makes writers like Parkin, who have the freedom and resumé to produce work for the world's biggest mainstream news sites, even more rare.

Game beat reporters. In our interviews in 2017, one writer was mentioned repeatedly as an exemplar of change: Cecilia D'Anastasio.[25] At that time, her peers indicated that she epitomized the role of a game beat reporter—a writer who covers a single game or game subject for a long period of time, cultivating knowledge and sources with the intent of having a steady stream of articles relating to that beat. Known then as *Kotaku's* "cyber sleuth," she went on to cover games for *Wired* before joining *Bloomberg Technology*.[26] During this period, D'Anastasio was most recognized for her long-standing work on game developers. Her essay for *Kotaku* on the sexist culture at Riot Games—the developer of the popular online game *League of Legends*—shook the industry, instigating employee strikes, lawsuits, an investigation by the California Department of Fair Employment and Housing, and, ultimately, improvements made by the company in reaction to the stories.[27] Not only was the article on a notoriously closed industry well researched and reported, but D'Anastasio followed up regularly after initial publication, filing updates, checking in with anonymous sources and counterbalancing company statements with employees' opinions and perspectives. This type of reportage has been atypical, to say the least. "The recent Riot investigation was excellent," one interviewee noted. "That's because [*Kotaku*] had someone who could spend six months doing it. [In] a mainstream publication, that's never going to happen."

Similar to enthusiast critics, *Kotaku's* investigative reporters occupy an incredibly exclusive table. Jason Schreier also sits among them; he is a former editor at the website, a journalist at *Bloomberg News*, and author of two popular books on the historically underreported subjects of game development and labor.[28] Game beat reporters like these follow franchises, companies, and games, particularly as the industry's business models moved from one-time purchases to ongoing services. Furthermore, they are employed by mainstream outlets and have made the medium itself a beat. We emphasize the notion of a "beat" because reporters follow the rigors of the job: garner sources, spot and break the next best story, maintain journalism's watchdog function, and hold those in power accountable.[29] The attitude of this category of writers is markedly closer to traditional journalists: "Journalistic integrity, that's what it comes down to," proclaimed one esports reporter. "You see a story and you need to present, even if it's not an argument, you need to balance so you're not just writing press releases." The upshot is a slew of articles not usually seen in enthusiast magazines or mainstream newspapers in terms of content and style. Rather than reviews, previews, or industry promotions, such work increasingly resembles Schreier's probes, including deep dives into the working conditions of Iranian game developers or the intrigues of the latest season of an esports competition such as the Overwatch League.[30]

The growth of game beat reporting has been driven in part by the enthusiast press's post-Gamergate overhaul. One game writer for a large enthusiast outlet stated that their employer decided "to stop focusing on games as products and start writing about them as essential cultural phenomena." Now working for more institutional outlets, this individual sees their writing as an effort to "see games as part of culture and therefore see them as part of the context of what's going on in the rest of the world as well." At enthusiast outlets, MacIntyre described "embedded writers" who wrote exclusively about "the developing community" around specific games, such as *Grand Theft Auto Online*. This shift in perspective took advantage of news outlets' strengths while expanding their writers' roles. In mainstream newsrooms that boast dedicated game beat reporters, striking a balance between traditional journalistic boundaries and gamers' subcultural norms is particularly difficult. Reporters' responsibilities entailed not only empathizing "with most people who play games—that is, people who have jobs, lives, families, and [are] able to sit there and play 300 hours of games a month," but also building trust between that group and more mainstream editors. As one writer/editor professed: "My boss doesn't know anything about games." It is both noteworthy and indicative of a clear shift toward cultural legitimacy that beat game reportage turns toward (rather than away from) journalistic norms.

Whether they are developing relationships for hard-hitting investigative pieces or simply focusing on games holistically, beat reporters elevate games beyond their entertainment value. Their stories expose the chicanery of industry politics, player experiences, and even the quotidian activities that surround digital play. This is not to say that beat reporters necessarily add to a common literacy. Like many other beat writers, it is their job to know characters and particulars that other people do not—just ask a local political reporter about community board meetings and you will get an earful. Game beat reporters must discern the information most relevant to a wider audience and reveal impropriety to instigate change. As with many beats across the United States, game beat reporters are few and far between. Sustaining their work on a budget is difficult. Ultimately, only a handful of prosperous outlets can dedicate so much time to a single game or subject while also dealing with potential backlash from avid fans.

Institutional journalists. In March 2020, as countless families were forced to shelter at home due to COVID's global spread, institutional newsmakers noticed the success of *Animal Crossing: New Horizons*. Released at the start of the pandemic, the game was chock full of wholesome activities, from socializing on friends' islands to maintaining a home. A mixture of glee and surprise accompanied articles, which suggested, with almost breathless wonder, that games might be *helpful* during the pandemic, and that parents should join their children in socializing online through gameplay.[31] Video games, along with other screens, could take on new importance during a period of social distancing.

Such coverage is hardly unique to institutional outlets. Each year, a game or two will cause a media sensation. When a game like *Pokémon Go* becomes an overnight phenomenon with millions of players crowding spaces (or worse), its story may suddenly fall within the bounds of traditional journalism. This may also explain why new installments of evergreen franchises such as *FIFA* (est. 1993) and *Call of Duty* (est. 2003) are largely ignored by the mainstream press; what else is there to comment on besides slightly improved graphics or gameplay?

In truth, game news often lies at the fringes of many of these institutions—not the center of an exclusive beat, but either lumped in with other reporting on business, science, and technology or tied to larger societal issues. They report on games only when a study comes out about video games and mental health; the question of games inciting violence is inevitably revisited after a school shooting; or the release of a new console draws attention from the tech section of institutional news sites. Thus, there is an abundance of publishers with an interest in games, but that interest and subsequent coverage is hardly consistent from outlet to outlet.

Institutional journalists, by contrast to their niche counterparts, tend to fall back on tried-and-true utopian and dystopian frames to characterize gameplay and ignore the cultural phenomena touted by game beat reporters, an attitude that is intimately connected to reader expectations.[32] "I can't have a slant," said one reporter. "I can't be an advocate for games and I cannot be against them either." They went on to describe how their reporting often had to have an angle: maybe educational benefits, or a sports association; even the World Health Organization's classification of a gaming disorder was cited. "If it's not hitting a mainstream audience, then I am not going to even pick up on it," former *Daily Beast* science editor Tanya Basu offered, later on stating that, for example, "a lot of tech addiction [stories] tend to do well." A business writer's overall pitch was that "this is a very big business, and it is worth paying attention to," but it was not quite as big as some other sectors that were on his plate. He added that the maturing of the industry, however, had caused a "bit of a mainstreaming effect." Thus, for each of these reporters, the choice of games was based on the perceived impact on the broadest possible audience, and a story lacking wide appeal could just as easily be nixed for another, more prominent topic.

As a result of this mix of indifference and preconceptions, institutional journalists themselves are stigmatized by those working in the game industry; one writer observed, "I have found that some people don't want to talk to me because I work for a big paper . . . Nobody thinks to give me tips." Mainstream reporters remain in a bubble, rehashing old arguments that much of the gaming media landscape moved on from long ago and lacking the ability to exert cultural influence in the vein of their enthusiast counterparts. For institutional reporters, professional boundaries can be surprisingly restrictive, yet their functions and impact are not minor: one of their cited goals is to introduce and show new audiences that gaming is an artistic entertainment medium. One editor at a legacy news outlet urged their game reviewers to evaluate games with respect to other media: "Is this as good as *Breaking Bad*? Should I play this game instead of going to this concert?" They added, "There's still a lot of people who don't know much about games . . . those people shouldn't be scoffed at." Such questions reinforce the traditional gatekeeping role of the journalist as a trusty intermediary to explain what makes games worthwhile to the broadest readership, thus perpetuating their public service role.

Across demographics, there is little question that institutional journalists hold the key to legitimation and being a ubiquitous source of game coverage. The imprimatur of major news outlets like the *Wall Street Journal* or *USA Today* can heavily impact how games are perceived in the public imagination.[33] Because they are bound within more traditional newsrooms, however, this category of writers supplies only a limited common literacy for games, relying on old frames rather than fostering new ones. For these writers, games remain an anecdotal rather than integral part of their daily work.

Many Streams Flowing in a Single Direction

Why, with such a profusion and variety of coverage, do even the most thoughtful critics consider the subject of games unsuitable for the front pages of major newspapers? For us, this chapter provides the start of an answer: despite the narrow focus of critics, game coverage is more diverse than ever before, with writers pushing the ubiquity, legitimacy, and literacy of gaming in ways that were previously inconceivable. Furthermore, editors are making efforts to both broaden and deepen coverage across a wide spectrum of outlets. At the same time, however, inherent tensions persist throughout the ecosystem in which journalists work. Most striking, writers are perpetually strapped for cash. We cannot emphasize enough the economic adversity they face as freelancers. Moreover, their precarity extends to ideology; according to our interviewees, game journalists often lack a clear path or vision as to what they are writing about. Harper Jay MacIntyre proposed that games moved from a child's toy to an "artistic medium" in the twenty-first century, and that "the tension between their role as consumer good and actual art hasn't been something that enthusiasts have really been able to reconcile yet, which means that I think it is harder at a mainstream website to push criticism." They echoed the ongoing discomfort game journalists feel about their position as cultural intermediaries. Other studies note game journalists' ongoing "ideology of anxiety" about their craft, which they describe as "the softest of the soft news."[34] Yet how could they have an unambiguous path when the journalistic landscape has also morphed, presenting a multitude of platforms and viewpoints that compete with their own for legitimacy?[35]

Institutional journalism and art criticism itself is said to be in perpetual economic crisis. There may be a few widely read national news publications, such as the *New York Times* or the *Washington Post*, but beyond these, players seem to inevitably turn to the enthusiast press or niche outlets that validate their own prerogatives, especially when the vocabulary and focus of the institutional press seems simplistic or generic by comparison. Indeed, the shifting sands of the news ecosystem is matched by the game industry's transformation. It was only recently that game publishers "started to embrace games as living things, games as service," according to MacIntyre, who further remarked, "but even then, that [view is] not long compared to what you get from football, right?" Another writer agreed that treating games more like "a service rather than a product just shipping out" required journalists to pay more attention than they once had. As the game industry keeps evolving, it refuses to settle upon clear norms and values, while constantly adapting its business models, technologies, forms, and formats. This mercuriality reflects the playfulness of the medium itself, which is also subject to constant experimentation and manipulation. But a lack of standards and shared vocabulary does not at all ease journalists' professional paths. Instead, it creates the perspectives we discussed at the beginning of the chapter: no matter how old they are, games remain ripe for constant reinterpretation by the next generation.

5
What It's Actually About

If there is one thing that unites game journalists, it is the profession's nomadic nature. Even the most successful writers ping-pong between outlets. This interviewee's experience is typical of most: After launching his career at a hometown alternative weekly newspaper that hoped game reviews would attract a younger readership, his progress was slow, steady, and varied. He freelanced at a bevy of print and online publications —such as (but not necessarily) *Rolling Stone*, *Wired*, *GamesRadar+*, and *Polygon*—paid by the word to churn out everything from listicles to long-form pieces. Yet, he was unable to secure the dream job of an editorship in this competitive landscape and persevered through gigs even as the verticals for which he wrote foundered and closed.[1] Like so many others, he could not exclusively cover games, so he expanded his portfolio to include other "geek" subjects, such as comics. This journalist had always wanted to write about games, but despite having gained significant institutional knowledge and access to some of the biggest studios, he was left treading water in a profession where permanent jobs are scarce.

In the previous chapter, we surveyed the environment that has contributed to game journalists' professional ambivalence in the post-Gamergate era. In this media landscape, opportunities to write about games abound while digital platforms engender precarious conditions in which news publishers and writers struggle to survive. Anyone can assume the mantle of "game journalist." Some may even find an audience in entertainment, niche, or mainstream channels. As the four archetypes discussed in the previous chapter illustrate, however, impediments to the legitimacy, literacy, and ubiquity of game writing endure. Game reporters are hardly a fixture of but rather migrate between outlets, whereas games, as a subject, are marooned outside the occupational ideologies and boundaries of institutional reporting. The game industry remains a de facto gatekeeper, its prerogatives and precedents restraining writers' entry and career paths.[2] Consequently, even though video game systems occupy three-quarters of US households, the question lingers: Why has game journalism not been accepted by mainstream media?

In this chapter, we identify the barriers, including the ephemeral place of journalists within newsrooms, that keep game journalism from joining the mainstream. As with the previous chapter, our observations are informed by interviewees who commented on their own challenges regarding game literacy, ubiquity, and legitimacy. We noticed that journalists were frustrated that each element necessary for uniform coverage was often undermined by vestiges of perennial controversies within the game journalism landscape. To make sense of these frustrations, we have identified three structural tensions that hinder mainstreaming. First, specialization challenges literacy. Writers continue to be preoccupied with tailoring their work to the core audience for whom the blockbuster-driven part of the game industry produces some of the world's most visible titles. Recall that, despite the industry's unrelenting growth, the specialized language and frames we delineated in the first half of the book hamper a more universal uptake, understanding, and language. Second, precarity challenges ubiquity. Google and Facebook, among other platforms, contribute to the financial insecurity that typifies the daily life of game journalists and constrains their ability to concentrate on more mainstream coverage. Finally, a lack of sincerity challenges digital play's legitimacy. In particular, mainstream publications consistently invalidate the medium through their refusal to treat games as worthy of serious coverage or hire game journalists as permanent staff. As we argued in the previous chapter, institutional support for game reporting, from either the game industry or news outlets, is haphazard and rare. After delving into each of these challenges more deeply, we can only conclude that game journalism deviates from a mainstream course. Therefore, in our concluding chapter we question both the direction and destination of mainstreaming, returning to our initial provocation: perhaps games will simply never enrich the front pages or arts sections of news sites.

Specialization Challenges Literacy

Early in the book, we discussed the need for literacy—a more universal understanding of the underlying mechanics and features of games, something on par with listening to rock music or reading a novel. Contemporary game journalism, however, still lacks consensus on what games are and do.[3] Authors treat them as specialized products intended not for a broader public but for a select audience: hardcore fans who, in turn, create the vernacular around games.

The notion of specialization pervaded our interviews—for instance, the insistence that games were growing up. Game writer Clayton Purdom stated that "appreciation for games" was an "age thing" with a "four- to five-year gap" between those who get them and those who do not. Audiences were considered either too young or too old for coverage beyond the limited scope of their favored publication. One writer was incredulous that struggling smaller newspapers would not cover games because they might attract other readers. "I don't think a ton of seventy-year-olds are reading our site," Jason Schreier similarly speculated when he wrote for *Kotaku*, adding later that there tended to be more of a "hardcore

focus" due to the site's blog-like nature. Several journalists suggested this kind of maturity was a major
stumbling block; as Simon Parkin put it, games were
"something you should put down when you become
an adolescent and maybe only pick up again when you
retire, aside from a few rounds of golf." It was partially
from this nostalgic viewpoint that Parkin has oriented
his work, asserting that "even if [players have] sort of
lapsed and they don't play games anymore, they'll
remember maybe interesting games they played while
they were at college, or whatever."

Writers' preoccupation with finding and maintaining an audience is counterbalanced by an enduring
distrust in them. Even if their numbers keep growing, new players are not considered to be well versed
in games. Readers are "smart and probably like other
cool things," according to Purdom, "but they might not
know a lot about games," so he had to find "broader
things" to write about during his stint at *Kill Screen*.
Another common theme was the fundamental belief
that games require a deep knowledge beyond that of
the general reader. Former *New York Daily News* reporter
Jason Silverstein simply asked, "At what point have you
engaged with a game long enough to be knowledge-
able about it?" Harper Jay MacIntyre opined that "the
rules of games are infinitely more arcane" than sports.
"Sports are made to be watched." Although most people
have some connection to sports, MacIntyre suggested
that "when you give someone a controller with 16-plus

buttons, the barrier to entry for games, for certain folks, makes it very difficult to talk about them." Others, such as Nick Paumgarten, the *New Yorker* contributor mentioned in chapter 1, claimed that it is more difficult to frame games—or situate their importance within journalistic and critical coverage—than it is with theater, film, and other art forms commonly followed by their publication's readership.

The result was what we think of as an "us versus them" mentality about games, where the perceived audience—mainstream or enthusiast—drove the stories. "The more mainstream the audience," said game writer and editor Rollin Bishop, "the more likely you don't have to skew toward what your traditional gaming audience might want to read because other people are going to read it." Whereas niche websites might emphasize game mechanics and skill, mainstream journalists resorted to such subjects as game addiction because past stories about children's health elicited favorable responses. We can safely say that writers cater work to their perceived audience's interests without seeking common ground between them.[4] And worse, this simply boiled down to, as one respondent told us, "stories you want to tell don't get told, purely based on the reality of the business."

Admittedly, the tilt toward more narrow literacies is not exclusive to game journalism. Professionals and scholars alike have lamented the collapse of a common language in the field.[5] Readerships are algorithmically sorted via social media platforms so only self-affirming content is served to them.[6] To thrive, newsmakers need to appease a more exclusive audience. Of course, styles often diverge based on outlet—a music review in *Rolling Stone* is very different from one in the *New Yorker*—and the contemporary news environment's platform dependency requires outlets to scrutinize readers' needs more closely to stay viable.

In the case of game journalism, appealing to readers requires attending to "core" audiences and the game industry, even if public perspectives are evolving. Feel free to disagree with us here, but the front pages of even the most progressive game websites still feature some of the same generic themes, including such recurring tropes as the ongoing "console wars," now being fought between Microsoft's Xbox Series X|S and Sony's PlayStation 5.[7] Catering to the concerns of core audiences leaves more casual fans behind; said Silverstein, "For most gamers, there's the system that they grew up with, and that's their kind of vision of gaming, and then ten years later people have an entirely different vision of it . . . The pace of change is so rapid." Thus, as cultural intermediaries, most game journalists remain the "passionate experts" we discuss in chapter 3. These experts stay attuned to the industry so they can inform the hardcore fans who justify their existence—a gordian knot that restricts consistent coverage.

Equally important, perspectives and ideas that might be the impetus for a common language about games are wanting. US academia turned out to be an important ally in constructing the artistic status of Hollywood films by establishing a canon and providing new generations of critics with a shared vocabulary.[8] Game scholarship, by contrast, has certainly contributed to ludic literacy and legitimacy, but has yet to have a similar impact.[9] Left to the purview of writers steeped in game capital—technical skills and past history with and knowledge of games—criticism and coverage can be difficult to comprehend, let alone be written for a general readership.

Precarity Challenges Ubiquity

Common language cannot be established when game journalists' employment always hangs in the balance.[10] For many writers, this is precisely the problem: they are not writing about games full-time. Freelancing, as we stated in the previous chapter, has increased the sheer number of articles about games in both mainstream and enthusiast outlets, but the economic precarity that comes with it and the constant quest for work prevents consistent coverage. Freelancing limits game journalists from establishing and internalizing professional norms and ethics and from finding cohesive benchmarks by which to practice their craft.

For those attempting to make a career covering games as freelancers, the situation is bleak. "Game journalists," one writer lamented, "are constantly overworked and underpaid in the process of doing all this work." In untenable positions, writers juggle multiple assignments to stay afloat financially. Time and again, freelancers bemoaned their insecurity and, unsurprisingly, many of them moved on to other jobs. One writer, exhausted after years of pitching stories without acquiring a solid gig, nearly gave up writing altogether. Another, frustrated by having to repeatedly chase editors for payments, went into promotions for an independent game studio. In fact, many of those we interviewed wound up pursuing jobs within the industry itself; examine the LinkedIn profiles of communications officers at game companies across North America and you will likely stumble upon more than a few former freelancers.

Occupational instability is further complicated by the economic precarity of news organizations more broadly. Print publications' shrinking budgets and consolidation by major conglomerates has simultaneously increased the need for and yet further devalued freelancers. The result is fewer long-form, investigative, or even historical pieces because of the costly nature of such work; the number of meetings with editors required (let alone travel expenses for face-to-face interviews, etc.) would increase a freelancer's billable time. A game editor for a mainstream paper noted that, despite the prestige of the position and their own eagerness to put in more time, they were only permitted to work three days a week because the publication did not have the resources to support a full-time position. Although freelancers may bring standout stories and perspectives to editors, they are not a fixture in newsrooms, arguably a key space where editorial decisions are made.

For most journalists aspiring to full-time, permanent jobs, their lowly position on the professional food chain perpetuates unpredictability in terms of payment and labor. Jason Schreier described the irregular paychecks during his freelancing days as "very stressful." Some freelancers writing for publications that folded were never paid at all; Chris Plante of *Polygon* admitted, "I still have dead companies that technically owe me money." As with careers in the game industry itself, there was and remains an expectation that merely gaining a foothold into the world of video games was compensation enough.[11] Beyond pay, labor was a dominant theme; Rollin Bishop remarked that one had to constantly "provide value to the editor by introducing them to [their] pitch," which would earmark a valuable story. Whether it was devoting excess hours to an investigative piece or just hustling for the next article, the notion of constantly working without pay was considered normal.

Game beat reporter Cecilia D'Anastasio—whose much-touted work in 2017 at *Kotaku* catapulted her career to *Wired*—exemplifies the nonfiduciary obstacles confronting freelancers. One reporter worried about the attacks D'Anastasio might face. "If one person is taking on all that kind of labor again, especially a woman, at some point someone's going to come for her, especially since she's reporting about corruption," the journalist said, adding, "I can't imagine what [D'Anastasio's social media] mentions look like." D'Anastasio had the backing of *Kotaku* for most of her reporting, but another freelancer might not be able to tackle a comparable investigation and be guaranteed the same protections. The increased visibility afforded by such platforms as Twitter, TikTok, and Facebook has made journalists —particularly ones who are members of marginalized groups—even more vulnerable.[12] Add to that the increased workload of freelancers engaging in constant "relational labor," or continuous work to connect with audiences across platforms.[13]

For freelancers, indulging in lofty, long-term projects typically takes a back seat because of the unrelenting imperative to score more work. As MacIntyre reminded us, "You can't expect a freelancer to work on something for three months unless you have the budget to do so, or it's a matter of access. It's much easier when you're actually a [full-time employee] of a site." The result is that freelancer precarity dissuades diversity in the profession. Workers who cannot tolerate insolvency, such as those supporting families, burdened by student debt, or simply lacking the savings to withstand a dry spell, cannot stay in it for long.

Consequently, novel modes, perspectives, stories, and ways of writing are stifled. The exertion of homogenous gamer voices was particularly evident after Gamergate, which famously forced some of the most talented writers to quit after enduring harassment.[14] To make matters worse, both news outlets and game publishers demonstrated a reluctance to publicly support those being harassed. MacIntyre declared that, since the controversy, game magazines remain "unable to adequately hold our art [i.e., games] accountable while also having our readers follow us across the line." On the more positive side, one editor described how the scandal compelled his publication to be bolder—but only after he and others faced significant disruption to their lives, such as the hacking of his wife's personal internet account and a subsequent FBI investigation. Like many others, he eventually left his job.

Beyond increased occupational risks, precarity affects the writing process itself. A freelancer's life promotes uncertainty about their craft. With the prevalence of different levels of ability, approach to the subject, and professional backgrounds, the quality of writing about games is erratic. Often, journalists simply do not have the time required to compose a meaningful review. It takes longer to go through all the levels of a game than to read a book, as Jason Silverstein reminded us, "so in some ways it's harder to cover than a lot of traditional beats because you just have to actually know the game inside and out. That's a very difficult thing to do just as far as time investment." Once again, passionate experts who already spend their free time playing core games are most primed to write about them. Noncore gamers, or even those who simply have other commitments, can hardly make a living in this environment.

One of the recurring themes in this book is the boundary work performed by traditional journalists. It is a process that functions to legitimize their collective occupation. Yet, in a position where success is always based on hustling for the next job, cultivating occupational boundaries and ideologies that might result in cohesive writing about games is nearly impossible. Such institutional support, though, is vital. Film scholar Mattias Frey convincingly argues that despite an ongoing public narrative of a "crisis" in their authority, film critics successfully fought to establish both their place within newspapers and criteria for evaluation that remains embedded even in the most watered-down online rating systems.[15] Game writers, by contrast, tend to lack such stability. They cannot fight for their place and are thus denied the kind of touchstone on which other modes of cultural criticism and reportage stand. Without institutional backing, there is no universal coverage—just more of it. More writing is not the same as ubiquitous narratives, which would make game journalism at least feel more mainstream.

Sincerity Challenges Legitimacy

Next to insufficient economic investment, a lack of emotional and intellectual investment also thwarts legitimacy in game journalism. Games are simply not taken seriously, especially at mainstream outlets. The topic does not conform to the expectations and beats of most newspapers and is therefore dismissed as frivolous or as not worth the hassle of dealing with aggressive fans. Such a view is reflected in the comments about games "growing up" that we discussed in the opening pages of this chapter. The implication is that the medium is still in its infancy. In comparing himself to film and music writers, Purdom confessed that he might not be taken seriously at a dinner party or be in the *Paris Review*. One author decried, "There's still always a large percentage of people [who] will say, 'This is stupid,' 'It's child's play,' always 'It's a waste of time.'" Games outside of children's entertainment "have this reputation for escapism, especially among enthusiasts," MacIntyre said, adding that "when you start to apply outside lenses or outside standards it starts to feel like sort of outsiders are knocking down the fort walls or kicking over your sandcastles." These statements reveal not only journalists' but also readers' skepticism about the sincerity of game journalism. MacIntyre also noted that coverage tends to be characterized by "fads of the time, because [games] tend to be more broadly understood as products" to consume, and when you're done with them, you get rid of them." By contrast, they said that football, for example, is not going to be replaced by a new type of football.

Games are continually framed by journalists as child's play, fad, or mode of escape. Without a common literacy surrounding them, publications struggle to situate them in any other way, and the industry's rapid growth and increasing diversity of content does not help. In fact, reporters acknowledged that if some "dreadful world event" or "political shift" happened, "that's the most important thing of the day and whatever you put out about video games just doesn't matter very much." But the insincerity goes deeper because, as the *New Yorker*'s Paumgarten acknowledged, there is a "legacy, a vestigial sense of gamers, of 'this is what boys do in the basement.'" Old tropes like these are surprisingly persistent. Aja Romano, a culture reporter at *Vox*, cautioned that it was also important "to really understand how that trope has functioned to sort of both alienate and demonize gaming culture and gamers over time."

The endurance of these contentions surprised us, especially when considering the more serious attempts by enthusiast journalists to find nuanced stories about the medium—something we expounded upon in the previous chapter. And for publications that foster this type of reporting—"elite" enthusiast sites such as *Kotaku* or *Polygon*—there were significant efforts toward legitimacy, whether it was the establishment of beat reporters or even formal codes of ethics. *Kotaku* is an insightful example. After many changes in ownership and years of posts about ethics, *Kotaku* now has a coherent editorial policy as an affiliate of G/O Media.[16] Among other things, it specifies that reporters "should pay our way when covering stories to avoid any suspicion of quid pro quo," and that freelance contributors must contractually agree to adhere to the same standards as staff writers.[17] Nevertheless, editorial policies across outlets are neither uniform nor necessarily inculcated into writers' professional lives in part because of their freelance status. Some are ignorant of publications' guidelines; one interviewee said principles were "internalized" rather than explicit. As is the case with most forms of journalism, ethical norms and direction stem not only from the rules of single publications but also from the general practices and perspectives of writers. It bears repeating that, ultimately, it is this lack of consensus among professionals that impedes legitimacy of the medium in the long run.

Even more immediate and ironic, the "core" fanbase around whom journalists have shaped content also stands in the way of the expansion of legitimate game coverage, making reporters' lives more difficult, especially those reporters who are visible on social media. The journalist and professor Evan Narcisse warned that "enthusiasts and the fan base can be a very prickly readership to serve because they have a lot of preconceived notions about what this job should be and how it happens. . . . People still think about payola as a thing in video game journalism." Simon Parkin, referring to Gamergate, relayed that the coverage about it "exasperated" fans' worst fears that journalists were just "campaigning against gamers" without "listening for the nuance." He noted that both fans and journalists have missed an opportunity to "show the wonderful diversity of the medium and how it's trying to explore games as a much richer and more interesting subject, beyond just 'Can I shoot the other guy before he shoots me?'" Instead, an article deemed "wrong" in the eyes of readers would earn him "a whole bunch of flaming," as another journalist put it. The ability of core audiences to reject different styles and perspectives, a necessary ingredient for legitimacy, is a constant frustration for writers. "Specialist games media readers don't tend to like it if we criticize games," said one enthusiast-turned–institutional reporter. "People don't tend to like it so much if you're like, 'This is exploitative,' or 'The way this game is made to encourage constant attention is not good.'" Even if legitimacy through criticism is a reporter's goal, it stays out of reach.

Given these obstacles, it is important to remember cultural legitimacy is not a naturally occurring process but rather one that is negotiated and at times even fought for. As we explained in the first half of the book, the mutual dependence between industry and journalism and the establishment of critical authority both play key roles in creating boundaries by which to assess media content. For instance, the television scholar Amanda Lotz demonstrated how by the 1980s, some thirty years after the medium gained widespread popularity in the United States, a more responsible form of reporting was already forming.[18] Critics who grew up watching TV "increasingly attended to investigations, reportage, and considerations of the business operations of this highly commercial industry, which deviated from the dominance of reviewing and emphasizing the artistic and aesthetic aspect of the medium that was more characteristic of their predecessors."[19] Lotz traces this development to a variety of factors, including technical and sociocultural changes and the creation of the Television Critics Association (TCA), which established a foundation for a unified identity and purpose behind critical authority in the face of challenges from new media environments. "[T]he collectivity of the group has aided the whole and helped to increase the significance and role of critics in the promotional practices necessary to cultural production."[20] In contrast to the more erratic world of game criticism, the joint institutional efforts of TV critics established legitimacy far beyond that of individual publications.

At the same time, Lotz argues, the legitimacy of TV criticism was also fostered by mutual dependence between networks and reporters. Like the press conferences and game conventions described in chapter 3, she details lavish studio "junkets" to curry journalists' favor toward specific shows.[21] In turn, critics acted as purveyors of the good and the bad in the next TV season. Eventually, these outings became places for critics and executives alike to hold the industry accountable even in the fragmented, high-pressure environment created by the growth of online news outlets like the ones we have covered in this book, which offered a greater diversity of content and style.[22] Sincerity, therefore, stemmed from the symbiosis between TV networks and the press.

Such critical authority and industry buy-in, however, are absent in gaming. Studios still tightly control the narrative around their games and utilize a wide array of promotional channels to disseminate their content. And with the flood of live streaming, they have avid fans who can showcase the latest and greatest games. "The way in which the gaming industry is structured," said Romano, "makes what would be 'mainstream gaming news' within game culture less accessible to mainstream media." Another game journalist and editor characterized the relationship between the press and the industry as precarious, with large publishers such as Bethesda Softworks reserving important announcements for major trade shows such as E3. One even speculated that access was overrated: "Publishers like to hoard, especially with mainstream game sites, access over us in ways that I don't think they even do with YouTubers or influencers who are much more interested in just taking whatever deals publishers actually give them."

A crisis of critical authority will only persist if writers must assert their importance while in constant negotiation with publications, readers, and the industry. This negotiation, however, can ultimately lead to the legitimation of a genre or medium. Outlets such as *Rolling Stone* likewise played a leading role in creating a common language around rock and roll music in the 1960s while positioning themselves as countercultural.[23] But even in these magazines, the relationship between editors and journalists can be testy. When studying the organizational hierarchy at music magazines in the United Kingdom, the music journalist and scholar Eamonn Forde found that freelancers are untethered from such structures and instead adhere to editors whose fixed physical presence within newsrooms allow them to control content.[24] These examples stress that despite infrequent conscious attempts, a fervent legitimation process is imperative for games to become mainstream.

Living on the Edge of Mainstreaming

Bereft of the building blocks of mainstream coverage, the vital stakeholders—journalists, publications, and consumers—are randomly molding impressions of games as they acculturate. When journalists write primarily for niche audiences, there is no common literacy. Ubiquitous coverage is challenged by the precarious situation of most writers, who must accede to the prerogatives of magazines and the industry to survive. Finally, and perhaps most important to our argument on mainstreaming, games are simply not taken seriously, with stakeholders continuing to consider them as immature. When industry and fans are less and less dependent on journalists, as seems to be the case with game journalism, establishing a mutual language, professional boundaries, and even job security all become daily challenges. And the cycle perpetuates itself—all of these problems are endemic, long-standing, and aggravated by the restructuring and shuttering of newsrooms and magazines across the United States. It is difficult to imagine how a common and mainstream approach to games can be cultivated under these circumstances.

So what recourse is there? Based on our interviews, a major concern revolves around the value of game journalists' labor. For individual writers, as we have demonstrated, it is difficult to make a career out of covering games. A would-be reporter or critic must truly love the craft, because their day-to-day efforts are defined by what Brooke Erin Duffy has theorized as "aspirational labor"; they must heavily invest in the niche culture and language of games to even begin to gain a foothold in the profession.[25] This necessitates playing hours of games without compensation, meeting publication deadlines for unpaid articles, and unswerving dedication to specific titles and genres to achieve even a modicum of success. At the same time, this army of aspirational writers can easily be replaced; as we noted at the beginning of the book, the proposition of playing video games for a living is quite seductive. This work, however, comes at the expense of institutional knowledge, occupational security, and ubiquitous, meaningful coverage. Until the value of game journalism is reconsidered, individual freelancers will soldier on without serious investment from mainstream outlets.

Coincidentally, while journalists find themselves in an unstable situation occupationally, publications themselves also teeter on the edge of legitimacy and stability in a fragmented media environment. They face competition from an industry that can easily and directly communicate with and promote its products to end users. Studios do not need to engage with news outlets the way other media industries do because they have immediate access to a well-heeled contingent of fans who will readily contribute to their bottom line. Film, music, and other media have relied on critics for legitimation, but a coherent dialogue about games between critics and consumers remains a pipe dream.

We have our flame-retardant clothing at the ready, so allow us to make a bold proposition: maybe game journalism should not be mainstream. Unlike staid sections of the newspaper, from local hard news to the arts, entertainment, and even sports, game journalism simply may not fit into a clearly defined category.[26] It might be more suitable to align games with lifestyle journalism, which, as a mode of service journalism, has a distinct market orientation but also conveys "real" information: "factual information and advice, often in entertaining ways, about goods and services [the reader] can use in their daily lives."[27] This purposefulness was echoed in our interviews: "Our job," said Harper Jay

MacIntyre, "is to share information as we get it that is either going to provide a service to our readers or is going to be something that they are interested in." The journalism scholar Folker Hanusch cites numerous subjects that fall under the lifestyle umbrella—fashion, health, technology, and gardening, among others—that appear in different sections of newspapers and websites.[28] He has dispelled academic critiques about this type of reporting "being unworthy of being associated with the term journalism."[29] He comments that the ties of "soft news" with commercialism are hardly unusual in the news landscape, which tends to define "hard news" primarily as reporting on violence and politics.

At the same time, mainstream outlets neither invest in game journalism nor indicate the degree to which games should be included in their bailiwick beyond vague nods to their unrelenting popularity. As a result, news organizations that wield the greatest power to check abuse in the game industry have little incentive to act as a watchdog. That said, the prominence of mainstream verticals such as the *Washington Post's* Launcher points to a promising future in which different forms of lifestyle journalism are embraced as essential categories for the long-term viability of newspapers. Unfortunately, even that well-received section was abandoned in 2023, accompanied by gaming staff layoffs. In hindsight, our interviewees were spot on: games and games reporting still have a lot of growing up to do.

6
Conclusion: Mainstream Is a Verb

Let us return to the questions with which we began this book: Do games need to be mainstream? Are they already? Industry professionals, journalists, critics, scholars, and others with vested interests unequivocally answer the first question "yes!" They substantiate our view that only through being mainstream can the culturally constructed constitutive ambivalences marking game culture be resolved. We disagree, however, with the notion that mainstreaming solely hinges on broader cultural acceptance, a logic that many peers and interviewees seem to internalize. For others, it is satisfactory for games to remain a niche interest for select communities to have a somewhat common framework and vocabulary to discuss and critique them. Mainstreaming should neither sacrifice ubiquity nor stifle journalists' efforts to help explain why play is meaningful and legitimate.

Regarding the second question, for some it is redundant: games are already mainstream. As part of an industry panel, game journalist Dean Takahashi argued that games "of course, are already mainstream, with titles like *Grand Theft Auto V* selling 90 million units and generating $6 billion in revenue."[1] Takahashi, in step with many colleagues, invoked the game industry's profound economic impact. Along with games' increased visibility in everyday life, this offers compelling evidence. Billions of dollars may signal ubiquity, even maturity, but economics do not paint the full picture. Are games akin to watching movies, or closer to gambling and adult entertainment? We cannot deny the significant financial footprint of the last two industries, but rarely do they receive consistent and meaningful mainstream coverage on their own terms. And it is not too much of a stretch to argue that porn, gambling, and games are all still perceived as deviant compared to other entertainment formats. The media scholar Ian Bogost, ever the provocateur, insists that "games are still a niche tricked by the echo chamber of internal success into thinking that they are approaching mainstream."[2]

Bogost's assertion coincides with our findings. In this book, we identified the widespread and deep influence of the game industry, essential for access, mediation, and a source of funding via advertisement. Historically, publishers shaped the nature of game coverage, and their impact remains largely unchanged in today's journalism landscape. If anything, the rise of streamers, creators, and entertainers, and their reliance on game makers and subcultural norms for success, perpetuates the insulation of public communication about games.

Twitch entertainers, for instance, even though they are not traditional reporters or even members of the enthusiast press, deal with many toxic issues ingrained in video game media while at the same time perpetuating the insular language surrounding gameplay.[3]

We also identified the enduring, critical role of journalists as cultural intermediaries who articulate mainstream appeal. That said, game publishers, the public, and even writers themselves remain ambivalent about the profession's role. Games may be played more than ever, but they are still treated as foreign entities without a common vocabulary, and coverage lacks consistent institutional support, even among well-funded enthusiast outlets. This presents a true conundrum: journalists take their work—the dissemination of news—seriously, and that attitude often seems incompatible with or antithetical to the frivolity and fun that are associated with digital play. Games simply seem to be too trite for the occupational ideology of traditional journalists, whose writing tends to be anything but playful.

In fact, other scholars have also observed the incompatibility between games and newsmakers.[4] In her critique of using "games" as a metaphor to describe interactive journalistic formats, the communications professor Sybil Nolan states that for skeptics, "news packaged like a game distracts the audience and keeps them away from more real communication with journalists."[5] It is precisely the intrinsic malleability and ambiguity of play that inhibit reporters' efforts to strive toward a more universal and objective "truth." Inherent issues such as these can only cause journalists further doubt as they dive into a subject that resists the very values that sustain their professional identities. Unfortunately, our results do not resolve these dilemmas. Instead, we find that game journalists sometimes meet and sometimes fall short of the challenges associated with advancing the standards for discourse about the medium. In many ways, our ambivalent position aligns with game journalists themselves, who occupy a professional field typified by occupational uncertainty, different vested interests, and fractured communities, all of which make it difficult to arrive at any easy or clear-cut conclusions.

We still want to offer at least a few pragmatic prescriptions for mainstreaming games in this chapter. To do so, we first provide some grounded yet aspirational solutions to the endemic problems presented in the book. Second, we confront our own sense of skepticism to imagine a future of game journalism in which, despite their ubiquity and economic might, games do not "grow up" or reach the mainstream. When we turn to the implications of our findings, this deviation from the mainstream hardly seems abnormal. Instead, the story of game journalism—particularly in the context of North American reportage—can be instructive for understanding and combating broader trends in a fragmented and niche media environment.

Practical Solutions for Game Journalism's Future

At the most elemental level, the way games are covered in terms of factors such as style and story assignments must advance along with the industry. As the industry continues to diversify the content it creates, game journalists should do the same with their reporting. Coverage will vary, sometimes resembling sports reportage and other times film criticism, and this inconsistent approach will continue to fuel game journalists' ambivalence about their jobs. They find themselves in an inscrutable situation: do they fall back on the subcultural norms of yesteryear, or forge ahead into the unknown? At the extremes, we find reporters who choose the former: entertainers, who tailor their work to gamers, and institutional journalists, who draw and observe strict ideological and occupational boundaries around the field. It is in the middle of the spectrum, however, where we find more nuanced and provocative forms of writing that unfortunately have neither the visibility nor the financial or occupational support to set the norms or define the genre that is game journalism.

Consequently, many avenues for game reporting appear paradoxical. The medium creeps into all forms of writing, from deep and personal reviews to hard hitting exposés to binge-worthy live streams and YouTube videos—all without a cohesive viewpoint. Dan Golding points to the murky gray areas that persist in the contemporary game writing environment as the driving factor behind this "decentralised and de-institutionalised" profession and its "poor levels of knowledge transference between established and emerging writers."[6] There may very well be areas of growth, maturity, and occupational diversity—we all frequently stumble upon thoughtful game stories from our most trusted news source—but the field lacks a solid, long-term foundation for coverage, thereby relegating the subject of games to the periphery of mainstream media. So, what are the potential solutions to smooth out this volatile situation? We offer six broad directives for writers and editors to consider.

First, game journalists should stop vacillating and instead steer themselves away from the position of the passionate expert and toward becoming a "journalist." The role of expert, which is so convenient to the industry, has use for entertainment purposes. There is little doubt that live streamers and content creators reinforce the former position. By doing so, entertainers directly challenge traditional publications and their place within the industry. Although they may cater to fans, antagonists such as PewDiePie are deemed problematic because they embrace their subcultural status. Conversely, game writers can tap into time-honored journalistic and critical traditions—from beat reporting, which thrives in traditional papers, to arts critics who still exert influence in magazines—by undertaking serious investigations into and interrogations of the industry, especially with regard to business models and labor abuses.

What particularly heartens us is mainstream and enthusiast outlets' growing focus on play and virtual communities. When considering how game coverage has changed since the COVID-19 pandemic began, we found that writers were concentrating less on specific platforms and more on the people that use them, an approach that often requires deep embedding.[7] When games such as *Animal Crossing: New Horizons*, *Minecraft*, and *Roblox* service hundreds of thousands of players daily and provide a bevy of tasks to complete and ways to play, it makes sense to emulate the style of on-the-street reporting. Crucially, this method of reporting can extend beyond individual titles.

Subtle shifts in professional orientation coincide with an equally challenging and ambitious second recommendation—in addition to taking a firm position on the spectrum between entertainer and journalist, we recommend that writers utilize the strengths of their profession to tell stories about games instead of seizing on meaningless buzzwords or minutiae such as graphic fidelity and distracting "technobabble," all of which typified writing by the early enthusiast press.[8] Whether a simple puzzle game or an intricate open-world RPG, games vary so wildly that concerns about the intricacies of specific franchises are frankly unimportant. Journalists should instead write about all facets of play. In a person-centered profession that cultivates sources, elicits quotes, and so on, individual titles may be less materially important for mainstreaming than a focus on the messiness of meaning making.[9] We ultimately think audiences can learn to (and often already do) read between the lines of gameplay to reach deeper meaning.

A move toward play-centered writing in practice means a further codification and communication of ethical and occupational norms by publications themselves, which brings us to our third and perhaps most practical recommendation: clearly broadcasting journalistic standards. We and other scholars have remarked how this sort of ethical transparency is assumed and internalized by many writers.[10] Editors' and writers' understanding of these rules, however, will always differ from one publication to another. As outlets expand their ethical guidelines, it is vital that they communicate requirements to writers, and that includes incorporating them into the onboarding and management of freelance staff. Closing the gap between editorial and freelance assumptions about ethics is a necessary step for building a bulwark against industry influence. It is publications with deeper pockets who can lead the way in standardizing such norms across game coverage.

Transparency in standardization can extend to occupational norms as well, which brings us to our fourth recommendation. Having more permanent and structured employment can only benefit game coverage as the medium's popularity expands. One of the most persistent concerns among our interviewees was the precarity of freelancing, which, as we wrote in chapters 4 and 5, was often a source of frustration. How can writers hone their craft and proceed with their jobs when they must constantly hustle for their next paycheck? This economic instability has often restricted game journalism to the domain of die-hard fans who were already obsessed with games; alternatively, it was viewed simply as a young person's job, something they could do before starting a family and pursuing a "real," sustainable career. This situation is endemic to what the game researcher Ergin Bulut describes as the "ludopolitics" of the industry, which fosters an expectation that those involved will devote time to their work solely on the basis of their passion for gaming.[11]

However rare, the hiring of full-time reporters to exclusively follow games, as organizations such as the *Guardian* and the *Washington Post* have done, fulfills deep-rooted desires for labor security. Ludopolitics led to calls for unionization by developers, and similar collective action needs to be taken by game journalists. Whether it is instigated by a freelancers' union or the staff union at a particular publication, or by a professional cohort similar to the Television Critics Association mentioned in the previous chapter, the fight for occupational norms in addition to standardized pay and benefits will ideally pave the way for consistent coverage. We realize that this solution is a tall order in the current journalistic environment of consolidation and downsizing. It arguably even necessitates a reconceptualization of newsrooms, an issue beyond the purview of this book. There are, however, minor victories worth noting, including the unionization of workers at G/O Media (owner of *Kotaku*), who went on strike to fight for salary minimums, parental leave, and annual raises, among other benefits.[12] Hard-won accomplishments may not solve industry-wide problems, as game reporter Jason Schreier acknowledged in his departure from *Kotaku* for *Bloomberg News*,[13] but it would be irresponsible of us to not endorse this slow and steady change, however aspirational it may be.

Fifth, we recommend not pigeonholing those who cover games. Fears about institutional journalists parachuting into stories are certainly understandable, but we view the continued cross-pollination as beneficial. For instance, Kellen Browning—a moderate outsider to the enthusiast press—has leveraged the *New York Times*'s financial support and reputation for high-quality reporting to produce deep investigative pieces on Twitch, Discord, and specific game franchises for the paper. Likewise, the hiring of former ESPN reporter Jacob Wolf (among others) expanded the scope of *DotEsports*'s coverage, making it a regular source for happenings in competitive gaming even as ESPN's esports division shuttered.

Finally, along with rethinking who should cover games, game journalists need to reconsider what qualifies as a "real" game or "legitimate" play. Rather than a topic relegated solely to arts or entertainment, writers can mimic the practices and ideologies of their lifestyle and sports counterparts. Ideally, this means that writers would not separate content from issues of labor and industry, but would also take care not to treat gamers as an exceptional culture. Breaking down the boundaries between various modes of play is increasingly necessary to illustrate how our relationship to games is changing. Big-budget games such as *Elden Ring* and solo experimental endeavors such as the puzzle game *Wordle* can both be blockbuster hits and therefore warrant significant coverage. In practice, these two types of games—not to mention those described as mobile or casual—tend to be artificially segregated from each other. Ultimately, it should be recognized that the avid *Pokémon Go* fan, the hardcore *Call of Duty* enthusiast, and the board game player excited over an expansion of *Wingspan*, all occupy similar rather than rarefied terrain.

In the end, these recommendations promote more diverse coverage and emphasize the ubiquity, legitimacy, and literacy of games in everyday life. It is a sentiment that many stalwarts in the profession seem to share. What, then, are the consequences of these proposed changes, and what might the future of game journalism look like?

Unhappily Ever After? Games Are "All Grown Up," but Forever Niche

When we began this research in earnest over five years ago, our conversation quickly turned to what game journalism might look like in the years ahead. With Gamergate and similar events still fresh in the rearview mirror, we, much the same as our interviewees, wrestled with the profession's destiny: luminaries we deeply respected were abandoning the industry even as games were receiving more coverage than ever before.

As our research came to an end, the horizon of serious game journalism started to crystallize into two distinct trajectories. On the optimistic side, we glimpsed the possibility of a future where game journalism had, in fact, "grown up." Another generation of players is coming of age. The industry continues to increase in size and prosperity. The platform-dependent and fractured journalistic environment described in chapter 4 has, in its own way, fueled the growth of serious game coverage. From this optimistic viewpoint, game journalism's prospects are seemingly bright, boasting more legitimate content, writers, and professional standards. The medium could find some sense of normalcy as it resides within the boundaries of institutional journalism, either in lifestyle sections or at the core of the newsroom.

The implication of this glass-half-full line of thinking is that if game journalists just keep their heads down and ply their craft, writers will slowly and surely develop a more common literacy and, by virtue of their coverage, legitimacy. This rosier picture also suggests that audiences will come to appreciate traditional cultural intermediaries and their form of criticism over—or at least in addition to—the entertainment promoted by creators on YouTube, Twitch, and TikTok. Coupling criticism and entertainment would provide fans with a holistic understanding of meaningful play. Even more important, game publishers would be more respectful of and responsive to journalists by appealing to them as a vital force in the legitimation of the medium. Much as movie critics did with cinema, game journalists could then alter gaming's cultural hierarchy, leaving its subcultural roots behind to engage in the fraught work of advancing games as a legitimate form of art. Taking a cue from Hollywood's successful move toward the mainstream, the game industry could strengthen its ties with academia beyond game design programs; encourage various forms of "extracommercial" assessment, such as industry-independent festivals and awards; or fund more "prestige productions," which may not be financially lucrative in the short term but could broaden the potential pool of players in the long run.[14]

As we finished our first draft of the manuscript, however, we found ourselves gravitating to the other, less auspicious ending: one in which games never reach mainstream acceptance. They may be (or already are) ubiquitous, but literacy and legitimacy remain elusive. In fact, games' ambiguities—their complexity, myriad types of play, genres, cultures, and even methods of monetization—are difficult to articulate to the public. And if there is no common literacy for gameplay, why would there be for game journalism? Further, the niche status of games continues to work to the advantage of publishers and platform providers who reap the lucrative rewards of a core audience that sustains them. Game developers and readers also do not uniformly value those cultural intermediaries who are explicit about their progressive politics.

This less promising future suggests that game journalists must simply accept the medium's subcultural status. Enduring as "niche" would hardly be strange. We already mentioned adult entertainment and gambling, but we could include comic books, toys, or even YouTube streaming, none of which are deemed fully legitimate forms of entertainment. Nor do they have (for journalists, at least) a common literacy despite their ubiquity and economic success.

Even if we embrace games' subcultural status, we cannot deny the size and scope of the game industry. Its economic dimension alone deserves "mainstream" treatment, even if only to hold powerful actors accountable the way we would any other corporate behemoth. Similarly, the industry is well connected, if not fully integrated, with some of the most prominent companies and ventures in the world, including tech giants such as Apple, Microsoft, and Sony.[15] Games lead the media industries in terms of exploring novel business models, production tools, and techniques.[16] Production software, such as the game engine Unity, is increasingly used for other purposes, from auto design to virtual reality, implanting game ideologies and practices into a diverse array of industries.[17] These connections, however, come with their own set of problems. Blockbuster publishers have a contentious history of violating labor rights, particularly in their normalization of "crunch" time, which demands that employees work well beyond regular business hours to bring a product to market by the deadline, and similar forms of ludopolitics mentioned previously.[18] Topics such as these are worthy of scrutiny by journalistic institutions. It is up to reporters and critics of all stripes to fight for cultural relevance and acceptance, as has happened with television and film.

And there lies the predicament in our more pessimistic outlook. Without journalistic investment or fan and industry buy-in, the possibility of games "growing up" seems incredibly difficult to achieve, despite the aspirations of our interviewees. The mainstreaming of games is frustratingly contradictory for several reasons. Some are cultural; the history and industry that exist around games and their exclusionary tactics simply cannot be erased. In the same way that US filmmaking is inextricably linked with Hollywood, or that high art is associated with Picasso and Monet, games have developed within a very specific set of norms and ideologies, which are likely to persist over time. In other words, after decades of moving toward more niche audiences and specific types of gameplay, there is a deep bed of cultural knowledge about games that will continue to impact their literacy and legitimacy. Another problem concerns play, which is exclusive, contingent, and messy. Almost any game—even analog classics, such as chess or poker—demands specialized knowledge and is dependent on cultural norms that create a steep learning curve for outsiders. We might even posit that it is precisely the complications of play that make it difficult for any writer to explain the nuances between different titles and genres, even when ignoring their cultural, political, and economic trappings. Ultimately, this speaks to the idea that games and play tend toward smaller groups and don't have the "mainstream" appeal of other forms of mass media.

Is Anything Mainstream?

We just gloomily surmised why games will never be mainstream. Yet, how unusual is their coverage in our increasingly polarized media environment? The journalistic landscape we described in chapter 4 is hardly unique to gaming; in general, newsmakers vie with entertainers, social media, streamers, and niche sites for clicks and dollars. Game studies scholars have acknowledged that historically they have tended to cordon off their subject matter as exceptional.[19] Our media and entertainment, however, are increasingly reliant on games and their narrower approach to culture, audience, and economy, which leads to ever fewer forms of media being treated as mainstream phenomena.

From a journalistic perspective, perceptions of audience and the occupation itself deepen divides. After all, since the popularization of the World Wide Web, there have been over two decades of debate around the erosion of the public sphere into multiple conflicting publics.[20] Atomization is not always negative; it can give rise to diasporic and marginalized voices. It can also cause users to "take sides" when it comes to their media consumption. Increasingly, platforms seem to cater to this reality; apps such as Twitch serve individual streamers and their followers, thereby playing host to niche news producers located at the extreme political right and left, among other polarizing online figures.[21] From "filter bubbles" and echo chambers to modes of distribution, platform dependency tends to push audiences to the margins.

Newsmakers likewise concede that the readership for whom they write is shifting. Journalism scholar Jacob Nelson has observed the changes in how audiences are imagined in the contemporary moment, not as faceless masses but as customers whose wants must be satisfied. His work highlights the often combative, untrusting relationship that now exists between providers and consumers.[22] Ironically, the United States is experiencing both the collapse of regional and local reporting and rising distrust in national outlets. Consequently, the process of mainstreaming is more questionable than ever.

A better understanding of game journalism can offer answers. If we are living at a time when nothing seems to be mainstream, then games fit right in! They function as a template for understanding not only how mass media and affiliated audiences persist outside of the mainstream but also how such a situation can come to pass in the first place. As discussed in the first half of the book, the foundations of game journalism originate from the industry's specific intention to stray from broad appeal and instead cultivate an exclusive community around their emerging medium. This move toward exclusivity seems to resonate in the current media environment, where advertising dollars are targeted to ever smaller groups; the scandals surrounding Facebook's parent company Meta and how they grow, protect, and manipulate specific cohorts of users to retain that userbase on affiliated platforms eerily echo these choices.[23]

Games are also paradigmatic for comprehending the key role that a specific brand of journalism practiced in North America plays in either limiting or fostering the process of mainstreaming.[24] It is important to remember that institutional publications helped give rise to the enthusiast press by treating games as mere child's play, whether rewarding or deviant, and it helps explain why magazines like the *New Yorker* still struggle with how to explain games. As we have suggested, the traditional "serious" nature of (US) journalism, with its focus on "objective" reporting and the profession's constant need to self-promote to remain viable, clashes with the medium's subjective and frivolous nature.[25] Thus, game journalism can help us see through the cracks in what bubbles up into mainstream status on the front pages of major news sites, especially when considering that such topics as social media platforms and cryptocurrency may not adhere to the ideological bounds of the field.

Mainstream as a Verb, Not a Noun

To make sure we leave with a ray of hope, we can appreciate that even though game journalism may never be "ordinary," very little is. In fact, as described in chapter 4, we live in a world of many streams. We can think of "mainstream" less as a noun and more as a verb—an action to be reckoned with and a force that journalists play a key part in directing. They can push for the ubiquity, literacy, and legitimacy of gaming and reroute the flow of media coverage, moving away from its more harmful elements and industry ties toward more unifying, diverse, and meaningful interpretations of play in contemporary society. Together with our colleagues, we recognize, however, that there are ongoing concerns about what qualifies as "mainstream" in a culture dominated by oligopolistic actors, hegemonic norms, and cultures built around the privileged few at the expense of marginalized others.[26] But journalists' long-standing role as cultural intermediaries can connect games to diverse publics and show how they are played around the globe and for wildly different reasons. There may never be a day when games are a "mainstream" phenomenon, but as with so many components of our lives, it is writers who can communicate their everyday vitality.

Journalism is only half the story; the other half is to reconceive our perceptions of games and play. The days of denigrating digital gaming as abnormal, abhorrent, or child's play are antiquated and long gone. We all engage with digital gaming and have been doing so for decades. Truthfully, and hopefully, game journalism is realizing this, albeit slowly and haphazardly. Conversely, collectively overcompensating by tooting the ahistorical horn of techno-solutionism—how "games will change the world"—is equally unproductive. They never have, they never will, and that is *fine*. The best way writers can approach this already ubiquitous medium is to reemphasize the subjects and principles that matter to all journalists: draw upon connections between institutions, one's professional identity, and industry to succeed. Until then, and despite the medium's incessant evolution, when it comes to public acceptance, games and journalism will remain at odds.

Notes

Chapter 1

1. Hayley Tsukayama, "Everything You Need to Know about *Fortnite* and Why It's So Popular," *Washington Post*, April 3, 2018, https://www.washingtonpost.com/news/the-switch/wp/2018/04/03/everything-you-need-to-know-about-fortnite-and-why-its-so-popular/. Over the summer of 2018, at the height of the game's success, there were over 150 million players worldwide who watched others play on Twitch and YouTube Gaming by the hundreds of thousands. At that point, the game pulled in over $120 million in revenue per month for Epic Games.

2. Nick Paumgarten, "How *Fortnite* Captured Teens' Hearts and Minds," *New Yorker*, May 14, 2018, https://www.newyorker.com/magazine/2018/05/21/how-fortnite-captured-teens-hearts-and-minds.

3. Dmitri Williams, "The Video Game Lightning Rod," *Information, Communication & Society* 6, no. 4 (2003): 523–550.

4. Paumgarten, "How *Fortnite* Captured Teens' Hearts and Minds."

5. Paumgarten.

6. To read about the relationship between the game industry's culture of secrecy and its inability to draw on an institutional memory, see Casey O'Donnell, *Developer's Dilemma: The Secret World of Videogame Creators* (Cambridge, MA: MIT Press, 2014).

7. Andrew Przybylski and Netta Weinstein, "How We See Electronic Games," *PeerJ* 4 (2016): e1931. https://doi.org/10.7717/peerj.1931.

8. For example, see Amy Green, Ryan Green, and Josh Larson, *That Dragon Cancer*, Numinous Games, computer, 2016; Lucas Pope, *Papers, Please*, 3909 LLC, computer, 2013; Brenda Romero, *Train*, board game, 2009.

9. Laura Parker, "Inside Controversial Game That's Tackling the Holocaust," *Rolling Stone*, August 31, 2016, https://www.rollingstone.com/culture/culture-news/inside-controversial-game-thats-tackling-the-holocaust-251102/.

10. Graeme Kirkpatrick, *Computer Games and the Social Imaginary* (London: Polity, 2013), 39.

11. Kirkpatrick, 73.

12. Kirkpatrick, 6.

13. Brian McKernan, "The Morality of Play: Video Game Coverage in *The New York Times* from 1980 to 2010," *Games and Culture* 8, no. 5 (2013): 307–329; Felan Parker, "Roger Ebert and the Games-As-Art Debate," *Cinema Journal* 57, no. 3 (2018): 77–100.

14. Whitney Phillips and Ryan M. Milner, *The Ambivalent Internet: Mischief, Oddity, and Antagonism Online* (Cambridge: Polity, 2017), 6, 10.

15. José van Dijck, *The Culture of Connectivity: A Critical History of Social Media* (New York: Oxford University Press, 2013).

16. Adrienne Massanari, "#Gamergate and The Fappening: How Reddit's Algorithm, Governance, and Culture Support Toxic Technocultures," *New Media & Society* 19, no. 3 (2017): 329–346; Whitney Phillips, "It Wasn't Just the Trolls: Early Internet Culture, 'Fun,' and the Fires of Exclusionary Laughter," *Social Media + Society* 5, no. 3 (2019), https://doi.org/10.1177/2056305119849493.

17. Gregory Perreault and Tim Vos, "Metajournalistic Discourse on the Rise of Gaming Journalism," *New Media & Society* 22, no. 1 (2020): 159–176; Severin Justin Poirot, "The Self-Perception of Video Game

Journalism: Interviews with Games Writers Regarding the State of the Profession" (PhD diss., University of Oklahoma, 2019).

18. Maxwell Foxman and David B. Nieborg, "Between a Rock and a Hard Place: Games Coverage and Its Network of Ambivalences," *Journal of Games Criticism* 3, no. 1 (2016), http://gamescriticism.org /articles/foxmannieborg-3-1.

19. Thomas F. Gieryn, "Boundary-Work and the Demarcation of Science from Non-Science: Strains and Interests in Professional Ide-ologies of Scientists," *American Sociological Review* 48, no. 6 (1983): 781–795; Seth C. Lewis, "The Tension Between Professional Control and Open Participation: Journalism and Its Boundaries," *Information, Communication & Society* 15, no. 6 (2012): 841.

20. Tim Vos and Ryan J. Thomas, "The Discursive (Re)Construc-tion of Journalism's Gatekeeping Role," *Journalism Practice* 13, no. 4 (2019): 396–412.

21. Maarit Jaakkola, *Reviewing Culture Online: Post-Institutional Cul-tural Critique across Platforms* (Cham, Switzerland: Palgrave Macmil-lan, 2022), 136.

22. Foxman and Nieborg, "Between a Rock and a Hard Place."

23. On game developers, see O'Donnell, *Developer's Dilemma*. On journalism, see Mark Deuze, "What Is Journalism? Professional Iden-tity and Ideology of Journalists Reconsidered," *Journalism* 6, no. 4 (2005): 442–464.

24. For music journalism, see Eamonn Forde, "Journalists with a Difference: Producing Music Journalism," in *Media Organisation and Production*, ed. Simon Cottle (London: Sage, 2003), 113–130. For film journalism, see Mattias Frey, *The Permanent Crisis of Film Criticism: The Anxiety of Authority* (Amsterdam: Amsterdam University Press, 2014). For television criticism, see Amanda D. Lotz, "On 'Television Criticism': The Pursuit of the Critical Examination of a Popular Art," *Popular Communication* 6, no. 1 (2008): 20–36.

25. Note that we purposely exclude two types that are not aimed at the broader public. First, our categorization ignores academic

forms of game criticism. Although scholars have been quite prolific in engaging in this form of writing, we would argue that, as of yet, their impact on mainstream audiences is small. For an overview of scholarly game criticism, see Patrick Jagoda, "Videogame Criticism and Games in the Twenty-First Century," *American Literary History* 29, no. 1 (2017): 205–218. Second, our categorization does not include the trade press. For instance, *Game Developer* magazine and its online counterpart *Gamasutra* are undeniably an institutional touchstone for producers; however, as with academic game criticism, we excluded this type of reporting because we are interested in forms of writing that are aimed at a public audience rather than a professional one. For more research on this subject, see Amanda C. Cote and Brandon C. Harris, "The Cruel Optimism of 'Good Crunch': How Game Industry Discourses Perpetuate Unsustainable Labor Practices," *New Media & Society*, May 7, 2021, https://doi.org /10.1177/14614448211014213.

26. Ian Bogost, *How to Talk about Videogames* (Minneapolis: University of Minnesota Press, 2015), x.

27. Bogost, *How to Talk about Videogames*, ix.

28. Rebecca Carlson, "'Too Human' Versus the Enthusiast Press: Video Game Journalists as Mediators of Commodity Value," *Transformative Works and Cultures* 2, no. 1 (2009), https://doi.org/10.3983 /twc.2009.098. See also Howard D. Fisher, "Don't Let the Girls Play: Gender Representation in Videogame Journalism and the Influence of Hegemonic Masculinity, Media Filters, and Message Mediation" (PhD diss., Scripps College of Communication of Ohio University, 2012), https://etd.ohiolink.edu/apexprod/rws_etd/send _file/send?accession=ohiou1332372302; Gregory Perreault and Tim Vos, "The GamerGate Controversy and Journalistic Paradigm Maintenance," *Journalism* 19, no. 4 (2018): 553–569; Wannes Ribbens and Ruben Steegen, "A Qualitative Inquiry and a Quantitative Exploration into the Meaning of Game Reviews," *Journal of Applied Journalism & Media Studies* 1, no. 2 (2012): 209–229.

29. Patrick Prax and Alejandro Soler, "Critical Alternative Journalism from the Perspective of Game Journalists," in *DiGRA/FDG '16:*

Proceedings of the First International Joint Conference of DiGRA and FDG, vol. 13, Dundee, Scotland, 2016, http://www.digra.org/digital -library/publications/critical-alternative-journalism-from-the-perspec tive-of-game-journalists, 10.

30. Folker Hanusch, "Broadening the Focus: The Case for Lifestyle Journalism as a Field of Scholarly Inquiry," *Journalism Practice* 6, no. 1 (2012): 5. See also Elfriede Fürsich, "Lifestyle Journalism as Popular Journalism: Strategies for Evaluating Its Public Role," *Journalism Practice* 6, no. 1 (2012): 12–25.

31. Hanusch, "Broadening the Focus," 5.

32. Bogost, *How to Talk about Videogames*, x.

33. Adam Ruch, "Signifying Nothing: The Hyperreal Politics of 'Apolitical' Games," *Communication Research and Practice* 7, no. 2 (2021): 128–147.

34. Maarit Jaakkola, "Witnesses of a Cultural Crisis: Representations of Media-Related Metaprocesses as Professional Metacriticism of Arts and Cultural Journalism," *International Journal of Cultural Studies* 18, no. 5 (2015): 537–554.

35. The idea of "objective reviewing" is certainly confusing. This oxymoron is particularly popular among game fans who are wary of the "social justice talk" or industry critiques that are—or at least should be—hallmarks of game criticism. It is unclear to us how, other than solely listing a title's technical details or requirements, to "objectively" review a game.

36. In terms of followings, as of 2023, Markiplier has 2.4 million followers on Twitch and 34 million subscribers on YouTube. An international star, Fernanfloo has 45.6 million subscribers on YouTube. Freyline has a dedicated following for a single game (*Sea of Thieves*) which means she only has 9,800 subscribers on Twitch.

37. Tony Harcup, "'I'm Doing This to Change the World': Journalism in Alternative and Mainstream Media," *Journalism Studies* 6, no. 3 (2005): 361–374; Sara Platon and Mark Deuze, "Indymedia Journalism: A Radical Way of Making, Selecting and Sharing News?" *Journalism* 4, no. 3 (2003): 336–355.

38. Jason Toynbee, "Mainstreaming: From Hegemonic Centre to Global Networks," in *Popular Music Studies*, ed. David Hesmondhalgh and Keith Negus (London: Hodder Arnold, 2002), 159.

39. For a similar discussion of how cult movies and fandom are rife with ambiguities in their relationship towards "mainstream, commercial cinema," see Mark Jancovich, "Cult Fictions: Cult Movies, Subcultural Capital and the Production of Cultural Distinctions," *Cultural Studies* 16, no. 2 (2002): 306–322.

40. Shyon Baumann, *Hollywood Highbrow: From Entertainment to Art* (Princeton, NJ: Princeton University Press, 2008); Jancovich, "Cult Fictions."

41. Benjamin Woo, "Is There a Comic Book Industry?" *Media Industries Journal* 5, no. 1 (2018): 27–46.

42. On the issue of comprehension, consider also how games express ideas through play and playfulness: "the use of a game is not only determined by its design, but also by the player's motivations and choice of actions." Kristine Jørgensen and Torill E. Mortensen, "Whose Expression Is It Anyway? Videogames and the Freedom of Expression," *Games and Culture* 17, no. 7–8 (2022): 1007.

43. Emma Vossen, "On the Cultural Inaccessibility of Gaming: Invading, Creating, and Reclaiming the Cultural Clubhouse" (PhD diss., University of Waterloo, 2018), https://uwspace.uwaterloo.ca/handle/10012/13649, 15.

44. Toynbee, "Mainstreaming."

45. Michael Z. Newman and Elana Levine, *Legitimating Television: Media Convergence and Cultural Status* (New York: Routledge, 2012), 4.

46. Dal Yong Jin, *Korea's Online Gaming Empire* (Cambridge, MA: MIT Press, 2010).

47. Parker, "Roger Ebert and the Games-As-Art Debate," 84.

48. Foxman and Nieborg, "Between a Rock and a Hard Place"; Perreault and Vos, "Metajournalistic Discourse on the Rise of Gaming Journalism."

49. Miguel Sicart, *Play Matters* (Cambridge, MA: MIT Press, 2014).

50. Our tone, scope, and brevity recognize the goal of the MIT Press's Playful Thinking series to publish short, readable, and provocative books.

51. Daniel C. Hallin and Paolo Mancini, *Comparing Media Systems: Three Models of Media and Politics* (Cambridge: Cambridge University Press, 2004).

52. Samuel Coavoux, Manuel Boutet, and Vinciane Zabban, "What We Know About Games: A Scientometric Approach to Game Studies in the 2000s," *Games and Culture* 12, no. 6 (2017): 563–584; Paul Martin, "The Intellectual Structure of Game Research," *Game Studies* 18, no. 1 (2018), http://gamestudies.org/1801/articles/paul_martin; Thorsten Quandt et al., "Digital Games Research: A Survey Study on an Emerging Field and Its Prevalent Debates," *Journal of Communication* 65, no. 6 (2015): 975–996.

53. For example, Poirot interviewed 15 US-based game journalists, Perrault and Vos interviewed 17 English-speaking game journalists, and Ribbens and Steegen interviewed 8 Flemish game journalists.

54. We conducted 20 interviews with 19 subjects, which took place over the phone or in-person, with one respondent choosing to answer questions by email. One interview in 2014 inspired our work, but we returned to that respondent for a second interview in 2017. We stopped at 19 subjects as we quickly reached the point of saturation in our first rounds of interviews. All interviewees were briefed on the scope of our research and gave informed consent before our conversations and our interview protocols were reviewed by ethics boards at Columbia University, the University of Oregon, and the University of Toronto. We were mindful to recruit a diverse pool by considering race, gender, and outlet. We had some moderate success as roughly half of respondents wrote mostly for the enthusiast press and half for the institutional press. Some practicalities hindered this process, however; in particular, we observed a lower response rate among those from underrepresented groups. Anecdotally, journalists told us that members of these groups (women, people of color, and LGBTQ+) may have been wary of such requests post-Gamergate,

particularly ones coming from white men such as ourselves. Still, we made significant efforts to quote diverse voices throughout this text to make sure the gamut of cultural concerns was represented in our findings. We have anonymized those writers who chose to remain "off the record." Last, there are categories of writers that we did not reach out to because they work at the edge of what we consider game journalism; for instance, those who exclusively write guides and walkthroughs or work as PR and marketing professionals for game publishers. In this sense, our own "boundary work" and understanding of game journalism influenced the study and findings.

55. Shira Chess and Adrienne Shaw, "A Conspiracy of Fishes, or, How We Learned to Stop Worrying about #GamerGate and Embrace Hegemonic Masculinity," *Journal of Broadcasting & Electronic Media* 59, no. 1 (2015): 208–220; Torill Elvira Mortensen, "Anger, Fear, and Games: The Long Event of #GamerGate," *Games and Culture* 13, no. 8 (2018): 787–806.

56. Anastasia Salter and Bridget Blodgett, "Hypermasculinity & Dickwolves: The Contentious Role of Women in the New Gaming Public," *Journal of Broadcasting & Electronic Media* 56, no. 3 (2012): 401–416; Vossen, "On the Cultural Inaccessibility of Gaming."

57. Kishonna L. Gray, Bertan Buyukozturk, and Zachary G. Hill, "Blurring the Boundaries: Using Gamergate to Examine 'Real' and Symbolic Violence against Women in Contemporary Gaming Culture," *Sociology Compass* 11, no. 3 (2017): e12458.

58. Massanari, "#Gamergate and The Fappening"; Christopher A. Paul, *The Toxic Meritocracy of Video Games: Why Gaming Culture Is the Worst* (Minneapolis: University of Minnesota Press, 2018). However, toxic behavior is not unique to game communities and "can evidently occur in a range of cultural sites and through, and in relation to, an array of different cultural identities." Matt Hills, "An Extended Foreword: From Fan Doxa to Toxic Fan Practices?" *Participations* 15, no. 1 (2018): 108.

Chapter 2

1. Electronic Arts, "Battlefield 5 Official Reveal Trailer," May 23, 2018, YouTube video, 2:34, https://youtu.be/fb1MR85XFOc.

2. Nina B. Huntemann and Matthew Thomas Payne, eds., *Joystick Soldiers: The Politics of Play in Military Video Games* (New York: Routledge, 2009).

3. Thomas H. Apperley and Kishonna L. Gray, "Digital Divides and Structural Inequalities: Exploring the Technomasculine Culture of Gaming," in *The Video Game Debate 2: Revisiting the Physical, Social, and Psychological Effects of Video Games*, ed. Rachel Kowert and Thorsten Quandt (New York: Routledge, 2020), 41–52.

4. Mikolai Dymek, "Video Games: A Subcultural Industry," in *The Video Game Industry: Formation, Present State, and Future*, ed. Peter Zackariasson and Timothy L. Wilson (New York: Routledge, 2012), 34–55.

5. Shira Chess and Christopher A. Paul, "The End of Casual: Long Live Casual," *Games and Culture* 14, no. 2 (2019): 107–118; Amanda C. Cote, *Gaming Sexism: Gender and Identity in the Era of Casual Video Games* (New York: New York University Press, 2020).

6. Emma Vossen, "On the Cultural Inaccessibility of Gaming: Invading, Creating, and Reclaiming the Cultural Clubhouse" (PhD diss., University of Waterloo, 2018), https://uwspace.uwaterloo.ca/handle/10012/13649.

7. Mia Consalvo and Christopher A. Paul, *Real Games: What's Legitimate and What's Not in Contemporary Videogames* (Cambridge, MA: MIT Press, 2019).

8. David B. Nieborg, "How to Study Game Publishers: Activision Blizzard's Corporate History," in *Game Production Studies*, edited by Olli Sotamaa and Jan Švelch (Amsterdam: Amsterdam University Press, 2021), 179–195.

9. Mia Consalvo, *Cheating: Gaining Advantage in Videogames* (Cambridge, MA: MIT Press, 2007), 18.

10. Graeme Kirkpatrick, *Computer Games and the Social Imaginary* (London: Polity, 2013); Graeme Kirkpatrick, *The Formation of Gaming Culture: UK Gaming Magazines, 1981–1995* (Basingstoke, UK: Palgrave Macmillan, 2015).

11. Kirkpatrick, *Computer Games and the Social Imaginary*, 40.

12. Carly A. Kocurek, *Coin-Operated Americans: Rebooting Boyhood at the Video Game Arcade* (Minneapolis: University of Minnesota Press, 2015).

13. José van Dijck, *The Culture of Connectivity: A Critical History of Social Media* (New York: Oxford University Press, 2013).

14. Nick Montfort and Ian Bogost, *Racing the Beam: The Atari Video Computer System* (Cambridge, MA: MIT Press, 2009).

15. Michael Z. Newman and Elana Levine, *Legitimating Television: Media Convergence and Cultural Status* (New York: Routledge, 2012).

16. In the late 1980s, a similar process took place in the UK, as noted in Kirkpatrick, *Computer Games and the Social Imaginary*.

17. Kocurek, *Coin-Operated Americans*; Michael Z. Newman, *Atari Age: The Emergence of Video Games in America* (Cambridge, MA: MIT Press, 2017).

18. Everett M. Rogers, *Diffusion of Innovations*, 4th ed. (New York: The Free Press, 1995).

19. Amanda C. Cote, "Writing 'Gamers': The Gendered Construction of Gamer Identity in *Nintendo Power* (1994–1999)," *Games and Culture* 13, no. 5 (2018): 479–503.

20. Rogers, *Diffusion of Innovations*, 249.

21. Newman, *Atari Age*, 12.

22. Kirkpatrick, *Computer Games and the Social Imaginary*.

23. Media and communications scholars have used game magazines to great effect to substantiate claims about gender representation or "violent" game content. See, for example, Erica Scharrer, "Virtual Violence: Gender and Aggression in Video Game Advertisements," *Mass Communication and Society* 7, no. 4 (2004): 393–412.

24. Stephen Kline, Nick Dyer-Witheford, and Greig De Peuter, *Digital Play: The Interaction of Technology, Culture, and Marketing* (Montreal: McGill–Queen's University Press, 2003), 120.

25. Dominic Arsenault, *Super Power, Spoony Bards, and Silverware: The Super Nintendo Entertainment System* (Cambridge, MA: MIT Press, 2017).

26. Maarit Jaakkola, *Reviewing Culture Online: Post-Institutional Cultural Critique across Platforms* (Cham, Switzerland: Palgrave Macmillan, 2022), 85.

27. Jaakkola, *Reviewing Culture Online*, 8.

28. James Newman, *Playing with Videogames* (New York: Routledge, 2008); Consalvo, *Cheating*.

29. Kline et al., *Digital Play*, 120.

30. Cote, "Writing 'Gamers.'"

31. Rebecca Carlson, "*Too Human* versus the Enthusiast Press: Video Game Journalists as Mediators of Commodity Value," *Transformative Works and Cultures* 2, no. 1 (2009), §4.5, https://doi.org/10.3983/twc .2009.098.

32. Cote, "Writing 'Gamers.'"

33. Kirkpatrick, *Computer Games and the Social Imaginary*; Kirkpatrick, *The Formation of Gaming Culture*.

34. Kirkpatrick, *The Formation of Gaming Culture*, 105.

35. Arsenault, *Super Power, Spoony Bards, and Silverware*, 74.

36. Consalvo, *Cheating*, 27.

37. Severin Justin Poirot, "The Self-Perception of Video Game Journalism: Interviews with Games Writers Regarding the State of the Profession" (PhD diss., University of Oklahoma, 2019), 7.

38. Dan Golding, "Writing Games: Popular and Critical Videogame Writing over Time," *TEXT* 22, no. 49 (2018): 2.

39. Kieron Gillen, "The New Games Journalism," *Kieron Gillen's Workblog*, March 23, 2004. https://web.archive.org/web/2012053123 5659/http://gillen.cream.org/wordpress_html/assorted-essays/the -new-games-journalism/.

40. Golding, "Writing Games."

41. Maxwell Foxman and David B. Nieborg, "Between a Rock and a Hard Place: Games Coverage and Its Network of Ambivalences," *Journal of Games Criticism* 3, no. 1 (2016), http://gamescriticism.org/articles/foxmannieborg-3-1.

42. Gregory Perreault and Tim Vos, "Metajournalistic Discourse on the Rise of Gaming Journalism," *New Media & Society* 22, no. 1 (2020): 159–176

43. Newman, *Playing with Videogames*, 34.

44. Carl Therrien, *The Media Snatcher: PC/CORE/TURBO/ENGINE/GRAFX/16/CDROM2/SUPER/DUO/ARCADE/RX* (Cambridge, MA: MIT Press, 2019).

45. Carl Therrien and Martin Picard, "Enter the Bit Wars: A Study of Video Game Marketing and Platform Crafting in the Wake of the TurboGrafx-16 Launch," *New Media & Society* 18, no. 10 (2016): 2328.

46. Brendan Keogh, "From Aggressively Formalised to Intensely In/Formalised: Accounting for a Wider Range of Videogame Development Practices," *Creative Industries Journal* 12, no. 1 (2019): 22.

47. Kline et al., *Digital Play*.

48. Aphra Kerr, *The Business and Culture of Digital Games: Gamework/Gameplay* (London: Sage, 2006).

49. Kline et al., *Digital Play*, xxix.

50. Newman, *Playing with Videogames*.

51. Therrien and Picard, "Enter the Bit Wars."

52. Brendan Keogh, *The Videogame Industry Does Not Exist: Why We Should Think Beyond Commercial Game Production* (Cambridge, MA: MIT Press, 2023).

53. Dmitri Williams, "The Video Game Lightning Rod," *Information, Communication & Society* 6, no. 4 (2003): 523–550.

54. Williams, "The Video Game Lightning Rod," 543.

55. Brian McKernan, "The Morality of Play: Video Game Coverage in *The New York Times* from 1980 to 2010," *Games and Culture* 8, no. 5 (2013): 321.

56. Felan Parker, "Canonizing *BioShock*: Cultural Value and the Prestige Game," *Games and Culture* 12, no. 7–8 (2017): 739–763.

57. Patrick Jagoda, "Videogame Criticism and Games in the Twenty-First Century," *American Literary History* 29, no. 1 (2017): 208.

58. Consalvo and Paul, *Real Games*.

59. Shira Chess, "A Time for Play: Interstitial Time, Invest/Express Games, and Feminine Leisure Style," *New Media & Society* 20, no. 1 (2018): 105–121.

60. Ben Lindbergh, "Why Does the Mainstream Media Struggle to Cover Video Games?" *The Ringer*, October 25, 2019, https://www.theringer.com/2019/10/25/20929604/the-mainstream-media-is-not-playing-games.

61. Vossen, "On the Cultural Inaccessibility of Gaming."

62. Perreault and Vos, "Metajournalistic Discourse on the Rise of Gaming Journalism."

63. Lindbergh, "Why Does the Mainstream Media Struggle to Cover Video Games?"

64. Keogh, "From Aggressively Formalised to Intensely In/Formalised," 22.

65. Kirkpatrick, *Computer Games and the Social Imaginary*.

66. Dymek, "Video Games," 36–44.

67. Keogh, "From Aggressively Formalised to Intensely In/Formalised," 27.

Chapter 3

1. Vox Media, "Careers," accessed October 4, 2022, https://www.vox-media.com/pages/careers-jobs.

2. For a similar version of this story, see Severin Justin Poirot, "The Self-Perception of Video Game Journalism: Interviews with Games Writers Regarding the State of the Profession" (PhD diss., University of Oklahoma, 2019), 37.

3. Dean Takahashi, *Opening the XBox: Inside Microsoft's Plan to Unleash an Entertainment Revolution* (Roseville, CA: Prima, 2002); Dean Takahashi, *The XBox 360 Uncloaked: The Real Story Behind Microsoft's Next-Generation Video Game Console* (Arlington, VA: Spiderworks, 2006).

4. David McGowan, "*Cuphead*: Animation, the Public Domain, and Home Video Remediation." *Journal of Popular Culture* 52, no. 1 (2019): 21.

5. Dean Takahashi, "*Cuphead* Hands-On: My 26 Minutes of Shame with an Old-Time Cartoon Game," *VentureBeat* (blog), August 24, 2017, https://venturebeat.com/2017/08/24/cuphead-hands-on-my-26 -minutes-of-shame-with-an-old-time-cartoon-game.

6. Maxwell Foxman and David B. Nieborg, "Between a Rock and a Hard Place: Games Coverage and Its Network of Ambivalences," *Journal of Games Criticism* 3, no. 1 (2016), http://gamescriticism.org /articles/foxmannieborg-3-1.

7. Julian Matthews and Jennifer Smith Maguire, "Introduction: Thinking with Cultural Intermediaries," in *The Cultural Intermediaries Reader*, ed. Jennifer Smith Maguire and Julian Matthews (London: Sage, 2014), 1–9.

8. Pierre Bourdieu, *Distinction: A Social Critique of the Judgement of Taste* (Cambridge, MA: Harvard University Press, 1984).

9. Mia Consalvo, *Cheating: Gaining Advantage in Videogames* (Cambridge, MA: MIT Press, 2007).

10. Shyon Baumann, *Hollywood Highbrow: From Entertainment to Art* (Princeton, NJ: Princeton University Press, 2008).

11. Jesper Juul, *A Casual Revolution: Reinventing Video Games and Their Players* (Cambridge, MA: MIT Press, 2010).

12. Takahashi, *The XBox 360 Uncloaked*.

13. "PlayStation Day 2008—Introduction Kaz Harai," YouTube video, 14:38, uploaded on February 10, 2011, by MenudaConsola, https://youtu.be/zEjJXAP3YAE.

14. In this chapter, the "I" and "me" refer to David Nieborg's experiences as a Dutch game journalist.

15. The newspaper was distributed for free at major public transportation hubs and was launched in early 2007.

16. Folker Hanusch, "Broadening the Focus: The Case for Lifestyle Journalism as a Field of Scholarly Inquiry," *Journalism Practice* 6, no. 1 (2012): 2–11.

17. Elfriede Fürsich, "Lifestyle Journalism as Popular Journalism: Strategies for Evaluating Its Public Role," *Journalism Practice* 6, no. 1 (2012): 12–25.

18. Poirot, "The Self-Perception of Video Game Journalism," 55.

19. Fürsich, "Lifestyle Journalism as Popular Journalism," 23.

20. Poirot, 92.

21. Rebecca Carlson, "*Too Human* versus the Enthusiast Press: Video Game Journalists as Mediators of Commodity Value," *Transformative Works and Cultures* 2, no. 1 (2009), §4.15, https://doi.org/10.3983/twc.2009.098.

22. David B. Nieborg and Tanja Sihvonen, "The New Gatekeepers: The Occupational Ideology of Game Journalism," in *Proceedings of the 2009 DiGRA International Conference: Breaking New Ground: Innovation in Games, Play, Practice and Theory*, vol. 5, Brunel University, London, UK, August 31–September 4, 2009, http://www.digra.org/wp-content/uploads/digital-library/09287.29284.pdf.

23. Howard D. Fisher, "Don't Let the Girls Play: Gender Representation in Videogame Journalism and the Influence of Hegemonic Masculinity, Media Filters, and Message Mediation" (PhD diss., Scripps College of Communication of Ohio University, 2012), https://etd.ohiolink.edu/apexprod/rws_etd/send_file/send?accession=ohiou

1332372302; Foxman and Nieborg, "Between a Rock and a Hard Place."

24. Mark Coddington, "The Wall Becomes a Curtain: Revisiting Journalism's News–Business Boundary," in *Boundaries of Journalism: Professionalism, Practices and Participation*, ed. Matt Carlson and Seth C. Lewis (New York: Routledge, 2015), 69.

25. Jamie Woodcock, *Marx at the Arcade: Consoles, Controllers, and Class Struggle* (Chicago: Haymarket Books, 2019), 89.

26. Jennifer Smith Maguire, "Bourdieu on Cultural Intermediaries," in *The Cultural Intermediaries Reader*, ed. Jennifer Smith Maguire and Julian Matthews (London: Sage, 2014), 22.

27. Mia Consalvo and Christopher A. Paul, *Real Games: What's Legitimate and What's Not in Contemporary Videogames* (Cambridge, MA: MIT Press, 2019), 61–86.

28. Peter Suderman, "*Red Dead Redemption 2* Is True Art," *New York Times*, November 23, 2018. https://www.nytimes.com/2018/11/23 /opinion/sunday/red-dead-redemption-2-fallout-76-video-games.html.

29. Suderman, "*Red Dead Redemption 2* Is True Art."

30. Christopher A. Paul, *The Toxic Meritocracy of Video Games: Why Gaming Culture Is the Worst* (Minneapolis: University of Minnesota Press, 2018).

31. Dean Takahashi, "Our Cuphead Runneth Over," *VentureBeat* (blog), September 8, 2017, https://venturebeat.com/2017/09/08/the -deanbeat-our-cuphead-runneth-over.

32. Adrienne Shaw, *Gaming at the Edge: Sexuality and Gender at the Margins of Gamer Culture* (Minneapolis: University of Minnesota Press, 2014), 4.

33. Russ Pitts, *Sex, Drugs, and Cartoon Violence: My Decade as a Video Game Journalist* (n.p.: Flying Saucer Media, 2016), 64.

34. Eric N. Bailey, Kazunori Miyata, and Tetsuhiko Yoshida, "Gender Composition of Teams and Studios in Video Game Development," *Games and Culture* 16, no. 1 (2021): 42–64.

35. Brooke Erin Duffy, *(Not) Getting Paid to Do What You Love: Gender, Social Media, and Aspirational Work* (New Haven, CT: Yale University Press, 2017), 33.

36. Nina B. Huntemann, "Working the Booth: Promotional Models and the Value of Affective Labor," in *Production Studies, The Sequel!* (New York: Routledge, 2015), 45.

37. Reflecting on his own decade long career as a game journalist, which ran from 2006 to 2016, mapping neatly with Pitts, David can only agree with this statement.

38. Pitts, *Sex, Drugs, and Cartoon Violence*, 135.

39. Consalvo, *Cheating*, 36.

40. Ramon Lobato and Lawson Fletcher, "Prestige and Professionalisation at the Margins of the Journalistic Field: The Case of Music Writers," in *Amateur Media: Social, Cultural and Legal Perspectives*, ed. Dan Hunter, Ramon Lobato, Megan Richardson, and Julian Thomas (London: Routledge, 2012), 122.

41. Gregory Perreault and Tim Vos, "Metajournalistic Discourse on the Rise of Gaming Journalism," *New Media & Society* 22, no. 1 (2020): 159.

42. Howard D. Fisher and Sufyan Mohammed-Baksh, "Video Game Journalism and the Ideology of Anxiety: Implications for Effective Reporting in Niche Industries and Oligopolies," *Journal of Media Ethics* 35, no. 1 (2020): 45–59.

43. Fisher and Mohammed-Baksh, "Video Game Journalism and the Ideology of Anxiety," 57.

44. "Doxxing" aims to reveal a target's personal information (e.g., addresses), whereas "SWATting" involves summoning a heavily armed police team to a victim's location. To get a sense of the personal toll of one of Gamergate's key targets, see the harrowing memoir by Zoë Quinn, *Crash Override: How Gamergate (Nearly) Destroyed My Life, and How We Can Win the Fight Against Online Hate* (New York: PublicAffairs, 2017).

45. Amanda C. Cote, *Gaming Sexism: Gender and Identity in the Era of Casual Video Games* (New York: New York University Press, 2020), 180.

46. Kishonna L. Gray, "Intersecting Oppressions and Online Communities: Examining the Experiences of Women of Color in Xbox Live," *Information, Communication & Society* 15, no. 3 (2012): 411–428.

47. David Nieborg and Maxwell Foxman, "Mainstreaming Misogyny: The Beginning of the End and the End of the Beginning in Gamergate Coverage," in *Mediating Misogyny*, ed. Jacqueline Ryan Vickery and Tracy Everbach (Cham, Switzerland: Springer, 2018), 111–130.

48. Shira Chess and Adrienne Shaw, "A Conspiracy of Fishes, or, How We Learned to Stop Worrying about #GamerGate and Embrace Hegemonic Masculinity," *Journal of Broadcasting & Electronic Media* 59, no. 1 (2015): 208–220.

49. Torill Elvira Mortensen, "Anger, Fear, and Games: The Long Event of #GamerGate," *Games and Culture* 13, no. 8 (2018): 787–806.

50. Gregory Perreault and Tim Vos, "The GamerGate Controversy and Journalistic Paradigm Maintenance," *Journalism* 19, no. 4 (2018): 565.

51. We do not mean to suggest they are the only bulwark, but one of many institutions that struggled to keep up with Gamergate tactics.

Chapter 4

1. Keza MacDonald, "Things I've noticed since moving from specialist media to the Guardian," Twitter thread, May 8, 2018, 7:21 a.m. (EDT), https://twitter.com/kezamacdonald/status/993858436562595841.

2. Thomas Poell, David B. Nieborg, and Brooke Erin Duffy, *Platforms and Cultural Production* (Cambridge: Polity, 2022).

3. These declines include consolidation of local outlets into larger conglomerates and the loss of revenue streams (like classified ads) that papers tended to monopolize. For research into the digitization of newsrooms, see Rasmus Kleis Nielsen, "Economic Contexts of

Journalism," in *The Handbook of Journalism Studies*, 2nd ed., ed. Karin Wahl-Jorgensen and Thomas Hanitzsch (New York: Routledge, 2019), 324–340.

4. Poell et al., *Platforms and Cultural Production*; Rasmus Kleis Nielsen and Sarah Anne Ganter, *The Power of Platforms: Shaping Media and Society* (New York: Oxford University Press, 2022).

5. José van Dijck, Thomas Poell, and Martijn de Waal, *The Platform Society: Public Values in a Connective World* (New York: Oxford University Press, 2018).

6. Maarit Jaakkola, *Reviewing Culture Online: Post-Institutional Cultural Critique across Platforms* (Cham, Switzerland: Palgrave Macmillan, 2022).

7. For more, see T. L. Taylor, *Watch Me Play: Twitch and the Rise of Game Live Streaming* (Princeton, NJ: Princeton University Press, 2018).

8. Mark R. Johnson and Jamie Woodcock, "The Impacts of Live Streaming and Twitch.tv on the Video Game Industry," *Media, Culture & Society* 41, no. 5 (2019): 670–688.

9. *IGN* was ranked at #498 in global traffic as of February 2020 according to Alexa search statistics: https://web.archive.org/web /20200210054521/https://www.alexa.com/siteinfo/ign.com.

10. "Mission Statement," *Critical Distance*, last updated December 13, 2021, https://www.critical-distance.com/about/.

11. Maxwell Foxman and David B. Nieborg, "Between a Rock and a Hard Place: Games Coverage and Its Network of Ambivalences," *Journal of Games Criticism* 3, no. 1 (2016), http://gamescriticism.org /articles/foxmannieborg-3-1.

12. These findings are fairly ubiquitous in the English-speaking press, with examples in Australia, the United States, and Canada. For more, see Kathryn Hayes and Henry Silke, "The Networked Free-lancer? Digital Labour and Freelance Journalism in the Age of Social Media," *Digital Journalism* 6, no. 8 (2018): 1018–1028.

13. Ben Lindbergh, "Why Does the Mainstream Media Struggle to Cover Video Games?" *The Ringer*, October 25, 2019, https://www

.theringer.com/2019/10/25/20929604/the-mainstream-media-is-not
-playing-games.

14. Foxman and Nieborg, "Between a Rock and a Hard Place."

15. Nicole S. Cohen, *Writers' Rights: Freelance Journalism in a Digital Age* (Montreal: McGill–Queen's University Press, 2016).

16. This is an avenue of exploration where there is room for significant future research to counterbalance journalists' and audience impressions.

17. We must confess that we felt ambivalent about including Kjellberg. Since 2017, he has been embroiled in a string of controversies regarding his public behavior. While there are plenty of other popular Let's Play artists who have not been entangled in such ignominy, we concur with Dan Golding's observation that YouTube as an outlet for all kinds of game journalism is "a combatively regressive one, and one that may actively work against the gains that videogame criticism made in diversifying its base writers and intellectual frameworks in the late 2000s." Dan Golding, "Writing Games: Popular and Critical Videogame Writing over Time," *TEXT* 22, no. 49 (2018): 12.

18. Stuart Cunningham and David Craig, *Social Media Entertainment: The New Intersection of Hollywood and Silicon Valley* (New York: New York University Press, 2019).

19. For instance, Kjellberg has made fun of being paid to "sit on [his] ass." See BBC, "YouTube Gaming Star PewDiePie 'Earned $7m in 2014,'" July 8, 2015, https://www.bbc.com/news/technology-33425411.

20. Vicky McKeever, "This Eight-Year-Old Remains YouTube's Highest-Earner, Taking Home $26 Million in 2019," CNBC, December 20, 2019, https://www.cnbc.com/2019/12/20/ryan-kaji-remains-youtubes-highest-earner-making-26-million-in-2019.html.

21. For more on relational labor, see Nancy K. Baym, *Playing to the Crowd: Musicians, Audiences, and the Intimate Work of Connection* (New York: New York University Press, 2018). For more on entrepreneurial journalism, see Nicole S. Cohen, "Entrepreneurial Journalism and the

Precarious State of Media Work," *South Atlantic Quarterly* 114, no. 3 (2015): 513–533.

22. Brooke Erin Duffy, *(Not) Getting Paid to Do What You Love: Gender, Social Media, and Aspirational Work* (New Haven, CT: Yale University Press, 2017).

23. These numbers only went up with the rise of COVID-19; see Bijan Stephen, "The Lockdown Live-Streaming Numbers Are Out, and They're Huge," *The Verge*, May 13, 2020. https://www.theverge .com/2020/5/13/21257227/coronavirus-streamelements-arsenalgg -twitch-youtube-livestream-numbers.

24. Simon Parkin, "Fifa: The Video Game That Changed Football," *Guardian*, December 21, 2016. http://www.theguardian.com/tech nology/2016/dec/21/fifa-video-game-changed-football.

25. While this was not mentioned by any of our interviewees, D'Anastasio's name has also been invoked regarding the challenges of reporting on alleged abuse, specifically regarding some reporting of hers that involved a game developer. This developer subsequently requested that the website *Kotaku*, D'Anastasio's employer, remove interview material about them, which they eventually did.

26. Ethan Gach, "Goodbye to Cecilia D'Anastasio, Planeswalking Cyber Sleuth and Aspiring Palutena Main," *Kotaku*, December 5, 2019, https://kotaku.com/goodbye-to-cecilia-danastasio-planeswalking -cyber-sleu-1840247238.

27. See, for example, Cecilia D'Anastasio, "Inside the Culture of Sexism at Riot Games," *Kotaku*, August 7, 2018, https://kotaku.com /inside-the-culture-of-sexism-at-riot-games-1828165483.

28. Jason Schreier, *Blood, Sweat, and Pixels: The Triumphant, Turbulent Stories Behind How Video Games Are Made* (New York: Harper, 2017); Jason Schreier, *Press Reset: Ruin and Recovery in the Video Game Industry* (New York: Grand Central Publishing, 2021).

29. For basic tenets, see Melanie Magin and Peter Maurer, "Beat Journalism and Reporting," in *Oxford Research Encyclopedia of Communication* (Oxford: Oxford University Press, 2019).

30. Aron Garst, "Video Game Development in Iran: Limited Tools, Front Companies and a Specter of War," *Washington Post*, February 5, 2020, https://www.washingtonpost.com/video-games/2020/02/05/video-game-development-iran-limited-tools-front-companies-specter-war/.

31. Sean Gregory, "Don't Feel Bad If Your Kids Are Gaming More Than Ever. In Fact, Why Not Join Them?" *Time*, April 22, 2020, https://time.com/5825214/video-games-screen-time-parenting-coronavirus/.

32. Dmitri Williams, "The Video Game Lightning Rod," *Information, Communication & Society* 6, no. 4 (2003): 523–550.

33. Or, at least, this is what we believe. Few studies have measured how mainstream journalists cover video games beyond Williams's research. Future research should certainly take this question into account.

34. Howard D. Fisher and Sufyan Mohammed-Baksh, "Video Game Journalism and the Ideology of Anxiety: Implications for Effective Reporting in Niche Industries and Oligopolies," *Journal of Media Ethics* 35, no. 1 (2020): 45–59; Severin Justin Poirot, "The Self-Perception of Video Game Journalism: Interviews with Games Writers Regarding the State of the Profession" (PhD diss., University of Oklahoma, 2019), 55.

35. Poirot, "The Self-Perception of Video Game Journalism," 98. The author similarly finds that the rise of streaming and video platforms complicates perceptions of game journalism.

Chapter 5

1. *Rolling Stone*, for instance, closed their gaming website Glixel.com in 2017.

2. Casey O'Donnell, *Developer's Dilemma: The Secret World of Videogame Creators* (Cambridge, MA: MIT Press, 2014).

3. Maxwell Foxman and David B. Nieborg, "Between a Rock and a Hard Place: Games Coverage and Its Network of Ambivalences,"

Journal of Games Criticism 3, no. 1 (2016), http://gamescriticism.org /articles/foxmannieborg-3-1.

4. Correspondents considered first to whom they were writing and then adjusted content, counterbalancing audience metrics that have become pervasive in the news industry. This is a longstanding debate; see Jacob L. Nelson, *Imagined Audiences: How Journalists Perceive and Pursue the Public* (New York: Oxford University Press, 2021).

5. These concerns, tied to the media's part in culture wars, go back well over two decades. See, for example, Todd Gitlin, *The Twilight of Common Dreams: Why America Is Wracked by Culture Wars* (New York: Metropolitan Books, 1995).

6. Thomas Poell, David B. Nieborg, and Brooke Erin Duffy, *Platforms and Cultural Production* (Cambridge: Polity, 2022), 139–143.

7. For an excellent critique of hardware "generations" and "console wars," see Carl Therrien, *The Media Snatcher: PC/CORE/TURBO /ENGINE/GRAFX/16/CDROM2/SUPER/DUO/ARCADE/RX* (Cambridge, MA: MIT Press, 2019).

8. Shyon Baumann, *Hollywood Highbrow: From Entertainment to Art* (Princeton, NJ: Princeton University Press, 2008).

9. Dan Golding, "Writing Games: Popular and Critical Videogame Writing over Time," *TEXT* 22, no. 49 (2018): 1–17.

10. One might wonder if game journalists who are permanently employed have enough authority to contribute to a common language. Institutional game journalists seem to be less visible than streamers, who do not seem concerned about shared vocabularies and cultural legitimacy.

11. For studies of labor conditions in studios, see Ergin Bulut, *A Precarious Game: The Illusion of Dream Jobs in the Video Game Industry* (Ithaca, NY: Cornell University Press, 2020); and O'Donnell, *Developer's Dilemma*. The journalists we interviewed were acutely aware of this relationship.

12. Poell et al., *Platforms and Cultural Production*, 170–173.

13. Nancy K. Baym, *Playing to the Crowd: Musicians, Audiences, and the Intimate Work of Connection* (New York: New York University Press, 2018).

14. See David Auerbach, "Gaming Journalism Is Over," *Slate*, September 4, 2014, https://slate.com/technology/2014/09/gamergate-explodes -gaming-journalists-declare-the-gamers-are-over-but-they-are.html; Carolyn Cox, "Female Game Journalists Quit Over Harassment, #GamerGate Harms Women," *The Mary Sue*, September 4, 2014. https://www.themarysue.com/gamergate-harms-women/.

15. Mattias Frey, *The Permanent Crisis of Film Criticism: The Anxiety of Authority* (Amsterdam: Amsterdam University Press, 2014).

16. Stephen Totilo, "A Brief Note about the Continued Discussion about Kotaku's Approach to Reporting," *Kotaku*, August 26, 2014, https://kotaku.com/a-brief-note-about-the-continued-discussion -about-kotak-1627041269.

17. G/O Media, "G/O Media Editorial Policy," accessed July 27, 2020, https://g-omedia.com/editorial-policy/.

18. Amanda D. Lotz, "On 'Television Criticism: The Pursuit of the Critical Examination of a Popular Art," *Popular Communication* 6, no. 1 (2008): 20–36.

19. Lotz, "On 'Television Criticism,'" 27.

20. Lotz, 34.

21. Lotz, 27.

22. Lotz, 29.

23. Ramon Lobato and Lawson Fletcher, "Prestige and Professionalisation at the Margins of the Journalistic Field: The Case of Music Writers," in *Amateur Media: Social, Cultural and Legal Perspectives*, ed. Dan Hunter, Ramon Lobato, Megan Richardson, and Julian Thomas (London: Routledge, 2012).

24. Eamonn Forde, "Journalists with a Difference: Producing Music Journalism," in *Media Organisation and Production*, ed. Simon Cottle (London: Sage, 2003), 113–130.

25. Brooke Erin Duffy, *(Not) Getting Paid to Do What You Love: Gender, Social Media, and Aspirational Work* (New Haven, CT: Yale University Press, 2017).

26. These "staid parts" of the newspaper are hardly uniform, particularly in the digital environment. There is a wide variety of different sections of newspapers based on region, newspaper type, etc.

27. Folker Hanusch, "Broadening the Focus: The Case for Lifestyle Journalism as a Field of Scholarly Inquiry," *Journalism Practice* 6, no. 1 (2012): 2; Thomas Hanitzsch, "Deconstructing Journalism Culture: Toward a Universal Theory," *Communication Theory* 17, no. 4 (2007);.

28. Hanusch's focus has mostly been on travel journalism, where he found that even if not affiliated with an institution, writers will take on journalistic trappings. See Hanusch, "Broadening the Focus."

29. Hanusch, 2.

Chapter 6

1. Dean Takahashi, "Gaming Has Gone Mainstream, But It Still Has Room to Grow," *VentureBeat* (blog), May 10, 2018, https://venture beat.com/2018/05/10/gaming-has-gone-mainstream-but-it-still-has -room-to-grow/.

2. Ian Bogost, *How to Talk about Videogames* (Minneapolis: University of Minnesota Press, 2015), 185.

3. Twitch is richly researched, but this subject matter falls outside of the book's purview. See, for example, Bonnie Ruberg, Amanda L. L. Cullen, and Kathryn Brewster, "Nothing but a 'Titty Streamer': Legitimacy, Labor, and the Debate over Women's Breasts in Video Game Live Streaming," *Critical Studies in Media Communication* 36, no. 5 (2019): 466–481.

4. Raul Ferrer-Conill et al., "Playful Approaches to News Engagement," *Convergence* 26, no. 3 (2020): 457–469; Maxwell Foxman, "Play the News: Fun and Games in Digital Journalism" (New York: Tow Center for Digital Journalism, 2015), https://academiccommons .columbia.edu/doi/10.7916/D8DJ5SWB/download.

5. Sybil Nolan, "Journalism Online: The Search for Narrative Form in a Multilinear World" (paper presented at the 5th International Digital Arts and Culture Conference, RMIT University, Melbourne, Australia, May 2003), 5, https://citeseerx.ist.psu.edu/pdf/dbd915e5e1 f3510c4cb00325aca94af3ebc84b6c.

6. Dan Golding, "Writing Games: Popular and Critical Videogame Writing over Time," *TEXT* 22, no. 49 (2018): 13.

7. Maxwell Foxman, "Lessons for Journalists from Virtual Worlds" (New York: Tow Center for Digital Journalism, 2022), https://www.cjr.org/tow_center_reports/lessons-for-journalists-from-virtual-worlds.php.

8. "Technobabble" is a discursive trope deployed by game journalists that constitutes pseudoscientific banter about technological minutiae to bedazzle readers; see Dominic Arsenault, *Super Power, Spoony Bards, and Silverware: The Super Nintendo Entertainment System* (Cambridge: MIT Press, 2017), 78.

9. Kristine Jørgensen and Torill E. Mortensen, "Whose Expression Is It Anyway? Videogames and the Freedom of Expression," *Games and Culture* 17, no. 7–8 (2022): 997–1014. https://doi.org/10.1177/15554120221074423

10. Severin Justin Poirot, "The Self-Perception of Video Game Journalism: Interviews with Games Writers Regarding the State of the Profession" (PhD diss., University of Oklahoma, 2019).

11. Ergin Bulut, *A Precarious Game: The Illusion of Dream Jobs in the Video Game Industry* (Ithaca, NY: Cornell University Press, 2020).

12. GMG Union, "Support GMG Union," accessed June 28, 2022, https://gmgunion.com/victory.

13. Rebekah Valentine, "The Uncertain, Unflinching Future of Games Media," GamesIndustry.biz (blog), April 20, 2020, https://www.gamesindustry.biz/articles/2020-04-20-the-uncertain-unflinching-future-of-games-media.

14. Shyon Baumann, *Hollywood Highbrow: From Entertainment to Art* (Princeton, NJ: Princeton University Press, 2008), 53–110.

15. Thomas Poell, David B. Nieborg, and Brooke Erin Duffy, *Platforms and Cultural Production* (Cambridge: Polity, 2022).

16. David B. Nieborg, "Apps of Empire: Global Capitalism and the App Economy," *Games and Culture* 16, no. 3 (2021): 305–316; Joost van Dreunen, *One Up: Creativity, Competition, and the Global Business of Video Games* (New York: Columbia University Press, 2020).

17. Maxwell Foxman, "United We Stand: Platforms, Tools and Innovation with the Unity Game Engine," *Social Media+ Society* 5, no. 4 (2019), https://doi.org/10.1177/2056305119880177.

18. Bulut, *A Precarious Game*; Amanda C. Cote and Brandon C. Harris, "The Cruel Optimism of 'Good Crunch': How Game Industry Discourses Perpetuate Unsustainable Labor Practices," *New Media & Society*, May 7, 2021, https://doi.org/10.1177/14614448211014213.

19. Alex Gekker, "Against Game Studies," *Media and Communication* 9, no. 1 (2021): 73–83.

20. Zizi Papacharissi, "The Virtual Sphere: The Internet as a Public Sphere," *New Media & Society* 4, no. 1 (2002): 9–27.

21. Maxwell Foxman, Brandon C. Harris, and William C. Partin, "Recasting Twitch: Livestreaming Platforms and New Frontiers in Digital Journalism" (under review).

22. Jacob L. Nelson, *Imagined Audiences: How Journalists Perceive and Pursue the Public* (New York: Oxford University Press, 2021).

23. *Wall Street Journal*, "The Facebook Files: A *Wall Street Journal* Investigation," accessed June 29, 2022, https://www.wsj.com/articles/the-facebook-files-11631713039.

24. This is the case in Europe as well, to some extent, given David's account in chapter 3.

25. Michael Schudson, "The US Model of Journalism: Exception or Exemplar?" in *Making Journalists: Diverse Models, Global Issues*, ed. Hugo de Burgh (London: Routledge, 2006), 110–122.

26. Chess, Shira. *Play like a Feminist* (Cambridge, MA: MIT Press, 2020).

Bibliography

Apperley, Thomas H., and Kishonna L. Gray. "Digital Divides and Structural Inequalities: Exploring the Technomasculine Culture of Gaming." In *The Video Game Debate 2: Revisiting the Physical, Social, and Psychological Effects of Video Games*, edited by Rachel Kowert and Thorsten Quandt, 41–52. New York: Routledge, 2020.

Arsenault, Dominic. *Super Power, Spoony Bards, and Silverware: The Super Nintendo Entertainment System*. Cambridge: MIT Press, 2017.

Auerbach, David. "Gaming Journalism Is Over." *Slate*, September 4, 2014. https://slate.com/technology/2014/09/gamergate-explodes-gaming-journalists-declare-the-gamers-are-over-but-they-are.html.

Bailey, Eric N., Kazunori Miyata, and Tetsuhiko Yoshida. "Gender Composition of Teams and Studios in Video Game Development." *Games and Culture* 16, no. 1 (2021): 42–64.

Baumann, Shyon. *Hollywood Highbrow: From Entertainment to Art*. Princeton, NJ: Princeton University Press, 2008.

Baym, Nancy K. *Playing to the Crowd: Musicians, Audiences, and the Intimate Work of Connection*. New York: New York University Press, 2018.

BBC. "YouTube Gaming Star PewDiePie 'Earned $7m in 2014.'" July 8, 2015. https://www.bbc.com/news/technology-33425411.

Bogost, Ian. *How to Talk about Videogames*. Minneapolis: University of Minnesota Press, 2015.

Bourdieu, Pierre. *Distinction: A Social Critique of the Judgement of Taste.* Cambridge, MA: Harvard University Press, 1984.

Bulut, Ergin. *A Precarious Game: The Illusion of Dream Jobs in the Video Game Industry.* Ithaca, NY: Cornell University Press, 2020.

Carlson, Rebecca. "*Too Human* versus the Enthusiast Press: Video Game Journalists as Mediators of Commodity Value." *Transformative Works and Cultures* 2, no. 1 (2009). https://doi.org/10.3983/twc.2009.098.

Chess, Shira. "A Time for Play: Interstitial Time, Invest/Express Games, and Feminine Leisure Style." *New Media & Society* 20, no. 1 (2018): 105–121.

Chess, Shira. *Play like a Feminist.* Cambridge, MA: MIT Press, 2020.

Chess, Shira, and Christopher A. Paul. "The End of Casual: Long Live Casual." *Games and Culture* 14, no. 2 (2019): 107–118.

Chess, Shira, and Adrienne Shaw. "A Conspiracy of Fishes, or, How We Learned to Stop Worrying about #GamerGate and Embrace Hegemonic Masculinity." *Journal of Broadcasting & Electronic Media* 59, no. 1 (2015): 208–220.

Coavoux, Samuel, Manuel Boutet, and Vinciane Zabban. "What We Know About Games: A Scientometric Approach to Game Studies in the 2000s." *Games and Culture* 12, no. 6 (2017): 563–584.

Coddington, Mark. "The Wall Becomes a Curtain: Revisiting Journalism's News–Business Boundary." In *Boundaries of Journalism: Professionalism, Practices and Participation*, edited by Matt Carlson and Seth C. Lewis, 67–82. New York: Routledge, 2015.

Cohen, Nicole S. "Entrepreneurial Journalism and the Precarious State of Media Work." *South Atlantic Quarterly* 114, no. 3 (2015): 513–533.

Cohen, Nicole S. *Writers' Rights: Freelance Journalism in a Digital Age.* Montreal: McGill–Queen's University Press, 2016.

Consalvo, Mia. *Cheating: Gaining Advantage in Videogames.* Cambridge, MA: MIT Press, 2007.

Consalvo, Mia, and Christopher A. Paul. *Real Games: What's Legitimate and What's Not in Contemporary Videogames*. Cambridge, MA: MIT Press, 2019.

Cote, Amanda C. "Writing 'Gamers': The Gendered Construction of Gamer Identity in *Nintendo Power* (1994–1999)." *Games and Culture* 13, no. 5 (2018): 479–503.

Cote, Amanda C. *Gaming Sexism: Gender and Identity in the Era of Casual Video Games*. New York: New York University Press, 2020.

Cote, Amanda C., and Brandon C. Harris. "The Cruel Optimism of 'Good Crunch': How Game Industry Discourses Perpetuate Unsustainable Labor Practices." *New Media & Society*, May 7, 2021. https://doi.org/10.1177/14614448211014213.

Cox, Carolyn. "Female Game Journalists Quit Over Harassment, #GamerGate Harms Women." *The Mary Sue*, September 4, 2014. https://www.themarysue.com/gamergate-harms-women/.

Cunningham, Stuart, and David Craig. *Social Media Entertainment: The New Intersection of Hollywood and Silicon Valley*. New York: New York University Press, 2019.

D'Anastasio, Cecilia. "Inside the Culture of Sexism at Riot Games." *Kotaku*, August 7, 2018. https://kotaku.com/inside-the-culture-of-sexism-at-riot-games-1828165483.

Deuze, Mark. "What Is Journalism? Professional Identity and Ideology of Journalists Reconsidered." *Journalism* 6, no. 4 (2005): 442–464.

Duffy, Brooke Erin. *(Not) Getting Paid to Do What You Love: Gender, Social Media, and Aspirational Work*. New Haven, CT: Yale University Press, 2017.

Dymek, Mikolaj. "Video Games. A Subcultural Industry." In *The Video Game Industry: Formation, Present State, and Future*, edited by Peter Zackariasson and Timothy L. Wilson, 34–55. New York: Routledge, 2012.

Electronic Arts. "Battlefield 5 Official Reveal Trailer." May 23, 2018. YouTube video, 2:34. https://youtu.be/fb1MR85XFOc.

Ferrer-Conill, Raul, Maxwell Foxman, Janet Jones, Tanja Sihvonen, and Marko Siitonen. "Playful Approaches to News Engagement." *Convergence* 26, no. 3 (2020): 457–469.

Fisher, Howard D. "Don't Let the Girls Play: Gender Representation in Videogame Journalism and the Influence of Hegemonic Masculinity, Media Filters, and Message Mediation." PhD diss., Scripps College of Communication of Ohio University, 2012. https://etd.ohiolink.edu/apexprod/rws_etd/send_file/send?accession=ohiou1332372302.

Fisher, Howard D., and Sufyan Mohammed-Baksh. 2020. "Video Game Journalism and the Ideology of Anxiety: Implications for Effective Reporting in Niche Industries and Oligopolies." *Journal of Media Ethics* 35, no. 1 (2020): 45–59.

Forde, Eamonn. "Journalists with a Difference: Producing Music Journalism." In *Media Organisation and Production*, edited by Simon Cottle, 113–130. London: Sage, 2003.

Foxman, Maxwell. "Lessons for Journalists from Virtual Worlds." New York: Tow Center for Digital Journalism, 2022. https://www.cjr.org/tow_center_reports/lessons-for-journalists-from-virtual-worlds.php.

Foxman, Maxwell. "Play the News: Fun and Games in Digital Journalism." New York: Tow Center for Digital Journalism, 2015. https://academiccommons.columbia.edu/doi/10.7916/D8DJ5SWB/download.

Foxman, Maxwell. "United We Stand: Platforms, Tools and Innovation with the Unity Game Engine." *Social Media+ Society* 5, no. 4 (2019). https://doi.org/10.1177/2056305119880177.

Foxman, Maxwell, and David B. Nieborg. "Between a Rock and a Hard Place: Games Coverage and Its Network of Ambivalences." *Journal of Games Criticism* 3, no. 1 (2016). http://gamescriticism.org/articles/foxmannieborg-3-1.

Foxman, Maxwell, Brandon C. Harris, and William C. Partin. "Recasting Twitch: Livestreaming Platforms and New Frontiers in Digital Journalism." Under review.

Frey, Mattias. *The Permanent Crisis of Film Criticism: The Anxiety of Authority*. Amsterdam: Amsterdam University Press, 2014.

Fürsich, Elfriede. "Lifestyle Journalism as Popular Journalism: Strategies for Evaluating Its Public Role." *Journalism Practice* 6, no. 1 (2012): 12–25.

Gach, Ethan. "Goodbye to Cecilia D'Anastasio, Planeswalking Cyber Sleuth and Aspiring Palutena Main." *Kotaku,* December 5, 2019. https://kotaku.com/goodbye-to-cecilia-danastasio-planeswalking-cyber -sleu-1840247238.

Garst, Aron. "Video Game Development in Iran: Limited Tools, Front Companies and a Specter of War." *Washington Post,* February 5, 2020. https://www.washingtonpost.com/video-games/2020/02/05/video -game-development-iran-limited-tools-front-companies-specter-war/.

Gekker, Alex. "Against Game Studies." *Media and Communication* 9, no. 1 (2021): 73–83.

Gieryn, Thomas F. "Boundary-Work and the Demarcation of Science from Non-Science: Strains and Interests in Professional Ideologies of Scientists." *American Sociological Review* 48, no. 6 (1983): 781–795.

Gillen, Kieron. "The New Games Journalism." *Kieron Gillen's Workblog,* March 23, 2004. https://web.archive.org/web/20120531235659/ http://gillen.cream.org/wordpress_html/assorted-essays/the-new -games-journalism/.

Gitlin, Todd. *The Twilight of Common Dreams: Why America Is Wracked by Culture Wars.* New York: Metropolitan Books, 1995.

GMG Union. "Support GMG Union." Accessed June 28, 2022. https:// gmgunion.com/victory.

G/O Media. "G/O Media Editorial Policy." Accessed July 27, 2020. https://g-omedia.com/editorial-policy/.

Golding, Dan. "Writing Games: Popular and Critical Videogame Writing over Time." *TEXT* 22, no. 49 (2018): 1–17.

Gray, Kishonna L. "Intersecting Oppressions and Online Communities: Examining the Experiences of Women of Color in Xbox Live." *Information, Communication & Society* 15, no. 3 (2012): 411–428.

Gray, Kishonna L., Bertan Buyukozturk, and Zachary G. Hill. "Blurring the Boundaries: Using Gamergate to Examine 'Real' and Symbolic Violence against Women in Contemporary Gaming Culture." *Sociology Compass* 11, no. 3 (2017): e12458.

Green, Amy, Ryan Green, and Josh Larson. *That Dragon, Cancer*. Numinous Games. Computer. 2016.

Gregory, Sean. "Don't Feel Bad If Your Kids Are Gaming More Than Ever. In Fact, Why Not Join Them?" *Time*, April 22, 2020. https://time.com/5825214/video-games-screen-time-parenting-coronavirus/.

Hallin, Daniel C., and Paolo Mancini. *Comparing Media Systems: Three Models of Media and Politics*. Cambridge: Cambridge University Press, 2004.

Hanitzsch, Thomas. "Deconstructing Journalism Culture: Toward a Universal Theory." *Communication Theory* 17, no. 4 (2007): 367–385.

Hanusch, Folker. "Broadening the Focus: The Case for Lifestyle Journalism as a Field of Scholarly Inquiry." *Journalism Practice* 6, no. 1 (2012): 2–11.

Harcup, Tony. "'I'm Doing This to Change the World': Journalism in Alternative and Mainstream Media." *Journalism Studies* 6, no. 3 (2005): 361–374.

Hayes, Kathryn, and Henry Silke. "The Networked Freelancer? Digital Labour and Freelance Journalism in the Age of Social Media." *Digital Journalism* 6, no. 8 (2018): 1018–1028.

Hills, Matt. "An Extended Foreword: From Fan Doxa to Toxic Fan Practices?" *Participations* 15, no. 1 (2018): 105–126.

Huntemann, Nina B. "Working the Booth: Promotional Models and the Value of Affective Labor." In *Production Studies, The Sequel!*, 59–65. New York: Routledge, 2015.

Huntemann, Nina B., and Matthew Thomas Payne, eds. *Joystick Soldiers: The Politics of Play in Military Video Games*. New York: Routledge, 2009.

Jaakkola, Maarit. "Witnesses of a Cultural Crisis: Representations of Media-Related Metaprocesses as Professional Metacriticism of Arts and Cultural Journalism." *International Journal of Cultural Studies* 18, no. 5 (2015): 537–554.

Jaakkola, Maarit. *Reviewing Culture Online: Post-Institutional Cultural Critique across Platforms*. Cham, Switzerland: Palgrave Macmillan, 2022.

Jagoda, Patrick. "Videogame Criticism and Games in the Twenty-First Century." *American Literary History* 29, no. 1 (2017): 205–218.

Jancovich, Mark. "Cult Fictions: Cult Movies, Subcultural Capital and the Production of Cultural Distinctions." *Cultural Studies* 16, no. 2 (2002): 306–322.

Jin, Dal Yong. *Korea's Online Gaming Empire*. Cambridge, MA: MIT Press, 2010.

Johnson, Mark R., and Jamie Woodcock. "The Impacts of Live Streaming and Twitch.tv on the Video Game Industry." *Media, Culture & Society* 41, no. 5 (2019): 670–688.

Jørgensen, Kristine, and Torill E. Mortensen. "Whose Expression Is It Anyway? Videogames and the Freedom of Expression." *Games and Culture* 17, no. 7–8 (2022): 997–1014.

Juul, Jesper. *A Casual Revolution: Reinventing Video Games and Their Players*. Cambridge, MA: MIT Press, 2010.

Keogh, Brendan. "From Aggressively Formalised to Intensely In/Formalised: Accounting for a Wider Range of Videogame Development Practices." *Creative Industries Journal* 12, no. 1 (2019): 14–33.

Keogh, Brendan. *The Videogame Industry Does Not Exist: Why We Should Think Beyond Commercial Game Production*. Cambridge, MA: MIT Press, 2023.

Kerr, Aphra. *The Business and Culture of Digital Games: Gamework/Gameplay*. London: Sage, 2006.

Kline, Stephen, Nick Dyer-Witheford, and Greig De Peuter. *Digital Play: The Interaction of Technology, Culture, and Marketing*. Montreal: McGill–Queen's University Press, 2003.

Kirkpatrick, Graeme. *Computer Games and the Social Imaginary*. London: Polity, 2013.

Kirkpatrick, Graeme. *The Formation of Gaming Culture: UK Gaming Magazines, 1981–1995*. Basingstoke, UK: Palgrave Macmillan, 2015.

Kocurek, Carly A. *Coin-Operated Americans: Rebooting Boyhood at the Video Game Arcade*. Minneapolis: University of Minnesota Press, 2015.

Lewis, Seth C. "The Tension Between Professional Control and Open Participation: Journalism and Its Boundaries." *Information, Communication & Society* 15, no. 6 (2012): 836–866.

Lindbergh, Ben. "Why Does the Mainstream Media Struggle to Cover Video Games?" *The Ringer*, October 25, 2019. https://www.theringer.com/2019/10/25/20929604/the-mainstream-media-is-not-playing-games.

Lobato, Ramon, and Lawson Fletcher. "Prestige and Professionalisation at the Margins of the Journalistic Field: The Case of Music Writers." In *Amateur Media: Social, Cultural and Legal Perspectives*, edited by Dan Hunter, Ramon Lobato, Megan Richardson, and Julian Thomas, 127–140. London: Routledge, 2012.

Lotz, Amanda D. "On 'Television Criticism': The Pursuit of the Critical Examination of a Popular Art." *Popular Communication* 6, no. 1 (2008): 20–36.

MacDonald, Keza. "Things I've noticed since moving from specialist media to the Guardian." Twitter thread, May 8, 2018, 7:21 a.m. (EDT). https://twitter.com/kezamacdonald/status/993858436562595841.

Magin, Melanie, and Peter Maurer. "Beat Journalism and Reporting." In *Oxford Research Encyclopedia of Communication*. Oxford: Oxford University Press, 2019.

Maguire, Jennifer Smith. "Bourdieu on Cultural Intermediaries." In *The Cultural Intermediaries Reader*, edited by Jennifer Smith Maguire and Julian Matthews, 15–24. London: Sage, 2014.

Martin, Paul. "The Intellectual Structure of Game Research." *Game Studies* 18, no. 1 (2018). http://gamestudies.org/1801/articles/paul_martin.

Massanari, Adrienne. "#Gamergate and The Fappening: How Reddit's Algorithm, Governance, and Culture Support Toxic Technocultures." *New Media & Society* 19, no. 3 (2017): 329–346.

Matthews, Julian, and Jennifer Smith Maguire. "Introduction: Thinking with Cultural Intermediaries." In *The Cultural Intermediaries Reader*, edited by Jennifer Smith Maguire and Julian Matthews, 1–9. London: Sage, 2014.

McGowan, David. "*Cuphead*: Animation, the Public Domain, and Home Video Remediation." *Journal of Popular Culture* 52, no. 1 (2019): 10–34.

McKeever, Vicky. "This Eight-Year-Old Remains YouTube's Highest-Earner, Taking Home $26 Million in 2019." CNBC, December 20, 2019. https://www.cnbc.com/2019/12/20/ryan-kaji-remains-youtubes -highest-earner-making-26-million-in-2019.html.

McKernan, Brian. "The Morality of Play: Video Game Coverage in *The New York Times* from 1980 to 2010." *Games and Culture* 8, no. 5 (2013): 307–329.

Montfort, Nick, and Ian Bogost. *Racing the Beam: The Atari Video Computer System*. Cambridge, MA: MIT Press, 2009.

Mortensen, Torill Elvira. "Anger, Fear, and Games: The Long Event of #GamerGate." *Games and Culture* 13, no. 8 (2018): 787–806.

Nelson, Jacob L. *Imagined Audiences: How Journalists Perceive and Pursue the Public*. New York: Oxford University Press, 2021.

Newman, James. *Playing with Videogames*. New York: Routledge, 2008.

Newman, Michael Z. *Atari Age: The Emergence of Video Games in America*. Cambridge, MA: MIT Press, 2017.

Newman, Michael Z., and Elana Levine. *Legitimating Television: Media Convergence and Cultural Status*. New York: Routledge, 2012.

Nieborg, David B. "Apps of Empire: Global Capitalism and the App Economy." *Games and Culture* 16, no. 3 (2021): 305–316.

Nieborg, David B. "How to Study Game Publishers: Activision Blizzard's Corporate History." In *Game Production Studies*, edited by Olli

Sotamaa and Jan Švelch, 179–195. Amsterdam: Amsterdam University Press, 2021.

Nieborg, David, and Maxwell Foxman. "Mainstreaming Misogyny: The Beginning of the End and the End of the Beginning in Gamergate Coverage." In *Mediating Misogyny*, edited by Jacqueline Ryan Vickery and Tracy Everbach, 111–130. Cham, Switzerland: Springer, 2018.

Nieborg, David B., and Tanja Sihvonen. "The New Gatekeepers: The Occupational Ideology of Game Journalism." In *Proceedings of the 2009 DiGRA International Conference: Breaking New Ground: Innovation in Games, Play, Practice and Theory*, vol. 5. Brunel University, London, UK, August 31–September 4, 2009. http://www.digra.org/wp-content/uploads/digital-library/09287.29284.pdf.

Nielsen, Rasmus Kleis. "Economic Contexts of Journalism." In *The Handbook of Journalism Studies*, 2nd ed., edited by Karin Wahl-Jorgensen and Thomas Hanitzsch, 324–340. New York: Routledge, 2019.

Nielsen, Rasmus Kleis, and Sarah Anne Ganter. *The Power of Platforms: Shaping Media and Society*. New York: Oxford University Press, 2022.

Nolan, Sybil. "Journalism Online: The Search for Narrative Form in a Multilinear World." Paper presented at the 5th International Digital Arts and Culture Conference, RMIT University, Melbourne, Australia, May 2003. https://citeseerx.ist.psu.edu/pdf/dbd915e5e1f3510c4cb00325aca94af3ebc84b6c.

O'Donnell, Casey. *Developer's Dilemma: The Secret World of Videogame Creators*. Cambridge, MA: MIT Press, 2014.

Papacharissi, Zizi. "The Virtual Sphere: The Internet as a Public Sphere." *New Media & Society* 4, no. 1 (2002): 9–27.

Parker, Felan. "Canonizing *BioShock*: Cultural Value and the Prestige Game." *Games and Culture* 12, no. 7–8 (2017): 739–763.

Parker, Felan. "Roger Ebert and the Games-as-Art Debate." *Cinema Journal* 57, no. 3 (2018): 77–100.

Parker, Laura. "Inside Controversial Game That's Tackling the Holocaust." *Rolling Stone*, August 31, 2016. https://www.rollingstone.com /culture/culture-news/inside-controversial-game-thats-tackling-the -holocaust-251102/.

Parkin, Simon. "Fifa: The Video Game That Changed Football." *Guardian*, December 21, 2016. http://www.theguardian.com/technol ogy/2016/dec/21/fifa-video-game-changed-football.

Paul, Christopher A. *The Toxic Meritocracy of Video Games: Why Gaming Culture Is the Worst.* Minneapolis: University of Minnesota Press, 2018.

Paumgarten, Nick. "How *Fortnite* Captured Teens' Hearts and Minds." *New Yorker*, May 14, 2018. https://www.newyorker.com/magazine /2018/05/21/how-fortnite-captured-teens-hearts-and-minds.

Perreault, Gregory, and Tim Vos. "The GamerGate Controversy and Journalistic Paradigm Maintenance." *Journalism* 19, no. 4 (2018): 553–569.

Perreault, Gregory, and Tim Vos. "Metajournalistic Discourse on the Rise of Gaming Journalism." *New Media & Society* 22, no. 1 (2020): 159–176.

Phillips, Whitney. "It Wasn't Just the Trolls: Early Internet Culture, 'Fun,' and the Fires of Exclusionary Laughter." *Social Media + Society* 5, no. 3 (2019). https://doi.org/10.1177/2056305119849493.

Phillips, Whitney, and Ryan M. Milner. *The Ambivalent Internet: Mischief, Oddity, and Antagonism Online.* Cambridge: Polity, 2017.

"PlayStation Day 2008—Introduction Kaz Harai." YouTube video, 14:38. Uploaded on February 10, 2011, by MenudaConsola. https:// youtu.be/zEjJXAP3YAE.

Platon, Sara, and Mark Deuze. "Indymedia Journalism: A Radical Way of Making, Selecting and Sharing News?" *Journalism* 4, no. 3 (2003): 336–355.

Poell, Thomas, David B. Nieborg, and Brooke Erin Duffy. *Platforms and Cultural Production.* Cambridge: Polity, 2022.

Poirot, Severin Justin. "The Self-Perception of Video Game Journalism: Interviews with Games Writers Regarding the State of the Profession." PhD diss., University of Oklahoma, 2019.

Pitts, Russ. *Sex, Drugs, and Cartoon Violence: My Decade as a Video Game Journalist.* n.p.: Flying Saucer Media, 2016.

Pope, Lucas. *Papers, Please.* 3909 LLC. Computer. 2013.

Prax, Patrick, and Alejandro Soler. "Critical Alternative Journalism from the Perspective of Game Journalists." In *DiGRA/FDG '16: Proceedings of the First International Joint Conference of DiGRA and FDG,* vol. 13. Dundee, Scotland, 2016. http://www.digra.org/digital-library/publications/critical-alternative-journalism-from-the-perspective-of-game-journalists/.

Przybylski, Andrew, and Netta Weinstein. "How We See Electronic Games." *PeerJ* 4 (2016): e1931. https://doi.org/10.7717/peerj.1931.

Quandt, Thorsten, Jan Van Looy, Jens Vogelgesang, Malte Elson, James D. Ivory, Mia Consalvo, and Frans Mäyrä. "Digital Games Research: A Survey Study on an Emerging Field and Its Prevalent Debates." *Journal of Communication* 65, no. 6 (2015): 975–996.

Quinn, Zoë. *Crash Override: How Gamergate (Nearly) Destroyed My Life, and How We Can Win the Fight Against Online Hate.* New York: PublicAffairs, 2017.

Ribbens, Wannes, and Ruben Steegen. "A Qualitative Inquiry and a Quantitative Exploration into the Meaning of Game Reviews." *Journal of Applied Journalism & Media Studies* 1, no. 2 (2012): 209–229.

Rogers, Everett M. *Diffusion of Innovations.* 4th ed. New York: The Free Press, 1995.

Romero, Brenda. *Train.* Board game. 2009.

Ruberg, Bonnie, Amanda L. L. Cullen, and Kathryn Brewster. "Nothing but a 'Titty Streamer': Legitimacy, Labor, and the Debate over Women's Breasts in Video Game Live Streaming." *Critical Studies in Media Communication* 36, no. 5 (2019): 466–481.

Ruch, Adam. "Signifying Nothing: The Hyperreal Politics of 'Apolitical' Games." *Communication Research and Practice* 7, no. 2 (2021): 128–147.

Salter, Anastasia, and Bridget Blodgett. "Hypermasculinity & Dickwolves: The Contentious Role of Women in the New Gaming Public." *Journal of Broadcasting & Electronic Media* 56, no. 3 (2012): 401–416.

Scharrer, Erica. "Virtual Violence: Gender and Aggression in Video Game Advertisements." *Mass Communication and Society* 7, no. 4 (2004): 393–412.

Schreier, Jason. *Blood, Sweat, and Pixels: The Triumphant, Turbulent Stories Behind How Video Games Are Made*. New York: Harper, 2017.

Schreier, Jason. *Press Reset: Ruin and Recovery in the Video Game Industry*. New York: Grand Central Publishing, 2021.

Schudson, Michael. "The US Model of Journalism: Exception or Exemplar?" In *Making Journalists: Diverse Models, Global Issues*, edited by Hugo de Burgh, 110–122. London: Routledge, 2006.

Shaw, Adrienne. *Gaming at the Edge: Sexuality and Gender at the Margins of Gamer Culture*. Minneapolis: University of Minnesota Press, 2014.

Sicart, Miguel. *Play Matters*. Cambridge, MA: MIT Press, 2014.

Stephen, Bijan. "The Lockdown Live-Streaming Numbers Are Out, and They're Huge." *The Verge*, May 13, 2020. https://www.theverge.com/2020/5/13/21257227/coronavirus-streamelements-arsenalgg-twitch-youtube-livestream-numbers.

Suderman, Peter. "*Red Dead Redemption 2* Is True Art." *The New York Times*, November 23, 2018. https://www.nytimes.com/2018/11/23/opinion/sunday/red-dead-redemption-2-fallout-76-video-games.html.

Takahashi, Dean. *Opening the XBox: Inside Microsoft's Plan to Unleash an Entertainment Revolution*. Roseville, CA: Prima, 2002.

Takahashi, Dean. *The Xbox 360 Uncloaked: The Real Story Behind Microsoft's Next-Generation Video Game Console*. Arlington, VA: Spiderworks, 2006.

Takahashi, Dean. "*Cuphead* Hands-On: My 26 Minutes of Shame with an Old-Time Cartoon Game." *VentureBeat* (blog), August 24, 2017. https://venturebeat.com/2017/08/24/cuphead-hands-on-my-26-minutes -of-shame-with-an-old-time-cartoon-game/.

Takahashi, Dean. "Our *Cuphead* Runneth Over." *VentureBeat* (blog), September 8, 2017. https://venturebeat.com/2017/09/08/the-dean beat-our-cuphead-runneth-over/.

Takahashi, Dean. "Gaming Has Gone Mainstream, But It Still Has Room to Grow." *VentureBeat* (blog), May 10, 2018. https://venture beat.com/2018/05/10/gaming-has-gone-mainstream-but-it-still-has -room-to-grow/.

Taylor, T L. *Watch Me Play: Twitch and the Rise of Game Live Streaming*. Princeton, NJ: Princeton University Press, 2018.

Therrien, Carl. *The Media Snatcher: PC/CORE/TURBO/ENGINE/ GRAFX/16/CDROM2/SUPER/DUO/ARCADE/RX*. Cambridge, MA: MIT Press, 2019.

Therrien, Carl, and Martin Picard. "Enter the Bit Wars: A Study of Video Game Marketing and Platform Crafting in the Wake of the TurboGrafx-16 Launch." *New Media & Society* 18, no. 10 (2016): 2323–2339.

Totilo, Stephen. "A Brief Note about the Continued Discussion about Kotaku's Approach to Reporting." *Kotaku*, August 26, 2014. https:// kotaku.com/a-brief-note-about-the-continued-discussion-about-kotak -1627041269.

Toynbee, Jason. "Mainstreaming: From Hegemonic Centre to Global Networks." In *Popular Music Studies*, edited by David Hesmondhalgh and Keith Negus, 149–163. London: Hodder Arnold, 2002.

Tsukayama, Hayley. "Everything You Need to Know about *Fortnite* and Why It's So Popular." *Washington Post*, April 3, 2018. https://

www.washingtonpost.com/news/the-switch/wp/2018/04/03/every
thing-you-need-to-know-about-fortnite-and-why-its-so-popular/.

Valentine, Rebekah. "The Uncertain, Unflinching Future of Games Media." GamesIndustry.biz (blog), April 20, 2020. https://www
.gamesindustry.biz/articles/2020-04-20-the-uncertain-unflinching
-future-of-games-media.

van Dreunen, Joost. *One Up: Creativity, Competition, and the Global Business of Video Games.* New York: Columbia University Press, 2020.

van Dijck, José. *The Culture of Connectivity: A Critical History of Social Media.* New York: Oxford University Press, 2013.

van Dijck, José, Thomas Poell, and Martijn de Waal. *The Platform Society: Public Values in a Connective World.* New York: Oxford University Press, 2018.

Vos, Tim P., and Ryan J. Thomas. "The Discursive (Re)Construction of Journalism's Gatekeeping Role." *Journalism Practice* 13, no. 4 (2019): 396–412.

Vossen, Emma. "On the Cultural Inaccessibility of Gaming: Invading, Creating, and Reclaiming the Cultural Clubhouse." PhD diss., University of Waterloo, 2018. https://uwspace.uwaterloo.ca/handle
/10012/13649.

Wall Street Journal. "The Facebook Files: A *Wall Street Journal* Investigation." Accessed June 29, 2022. https://www.wsj.com/articles/the
-facebook-files-11631713039.

Williams, Dmitri. "The Video Game Lightning Rod." *Information, Communication & Society* 6, no. 4 (2003): 523–550.

Woo, Benjamin. "Is There a Comic Book Industry?" *Media Industries Journal* 5, no. 1 (2018): 27–46.

Woodcock, Jamie. *Marx at the Arcade: Consoles, Controllers, and Class Struggle.* Chicago: Haymarket Books, 2019.

Index

Page numbers in italics denote illustrations.